English for
Customer Care

EXPRESS SERIES

Rosemary Richey

OXFORD
UNIVERSITY PRESS

OXFORD
UNIVERSITY PRESS

Great Clarendon Street, Oxford OX2 6DP

Oxford University Press is a department of the University of Oxford.
It furthers the University's objective of excellence in research, scholarship,
and education by publishing worldwide in

Oxford New York

Auckland Cape Town Dar es Salaam Hong Kong Karachi
Kuala Lumpur Madrid Melbourne Mexico City Nairobi
New Delhi Shanghai Taipei Toronto

With offices in

Argentina Austria Brazil Chile Czech Republic France Greece
Guatemala Hungary Italy Japan Poland Portugal Singapore
South Korea Switzerland Thailand Turkey Ukraine Vietnam

OXFORD and OXFORD ENGLISH are registered trade marks of
Oxford University Press in the UK and in certain other countries

ISBN: 978 0 19 457907 0

Printed in China

ACKNOWLEDGEMENTS

Prepared for OUP by Starfish Design Editorial and Project Management Ltd

Cartoons by: Stephen May

Photo credits: istock photo library and Alamy

Cover images courtesy of: Getty Images (main image/Altrendo; top left/
Richard Drury/Image Bank) and Punchstock (bottom left/Stockbyte)

MultiROM

English for Customer Care is accompanied by a MultiROM
which has a number of features.

Interactive exercises to practise useful phrases, vocabulary,
and communication through your computer.

Listening extracts. These are in enhanced audio format that
can be played on a conventional CD-player or through the
audio player on your computer.

If you have any problems, please check the technical support section of the readme file on the MultiROM.

Contents

About the book

English for Customer Care has been developed for people working in customer service who need a good level of English. You might be working in the sales or customer service department of a company, or you might have direct contact with customers in a bank or hotel. Or perhaps you speak to customers on the telephone from a helpdesk or a call centre. In all of these situations you need language skills and specific techniques in order to be able to communicate successfully. **English for Customer Care** not only offers expressions and vocabulary, it also addresses strategies related to the effective use of English in a business context.

English for Customer Care consists of six units. The first unit offers an introduction to the basic principles of Customer Service. The following four units deal with various different forms of customer contact: face to face meetings, telephone calls, call centres, or written communication. The final unit presents speaking skills that are needed in order to solve problems and deal with customer complaints effectively.

Each unit begins with a **Starter**, which consists of small exercises, brainstorming activities, or a quiz. This is followed by dialogues, texts, and authentic documents, along with a variety of exercises that help you to learn the vocabulary and expressions in context. You will be directed to the **Partner Files** at various points in the units, where role-play information gap activities allow you and a partner to practise the language presented in the unit in realistic situations. Each unit ends with a text which relates to the topic of the unit and leads to discussion. When you have worked through all the units you can **Test yourself!** with a crossword on the vocabulary in the book.

The **MultiROM** contains all the **Listening extracts** from the book. These can be played through the audio player on your computer, or through a conventional CD-player. In order to give yourself extra listening practice, listen to it in your car or copy it to your MP3 player. The **Interactive exercises** let you review by doing exercises that cover the essential language from the book, this will be particularly valuable if you are using the book for self-study.

At the back of **English for Customer Care** there is an **Answer key** where you can check your answers. You will also find the **Partner Files**, the **Transcripts** of the listening extracts, an **A–Z word list**, and a list of **Useful phrases and vocabulary** that you can refer to while you are at work.

Introduction to customer care

People have strong opinions about customer care. What is important for you as a customer? Work with a partner to make a list of the kind of services you expect.

Notes

1 **Read about the importance of customer care in the article and find four word partnerships with *customer*.**

customer

Can you add any other words to make more partnerships?

Think about the most successful shopping sites on the Internet. What do they have in common? Whether you are booking a holiday, buying books and music or simply doing the weekly shop, the best sites provide the highest levels of customer satisfaction. How do they do it? Why is customer care such a priority?

For most shoppers, customer convenience is the most important factor. Up-to-date technology means that when you return to a site you have visited before, they will remember your name, your profile, and what you bought last time. They also track where you browsed and what you thought about buying. They can also make some recommendations about other places, titles, or products.

We demand customer-friendly navigation and the best sites provide it, continually raising their levels of service. Convenient and efficient payment systems are also essential.

Sometimes, of course, things go wrong but this is when the sites are even better at dealing with customers. You can call a helpline and talk to an agent, email your problem and get a reply within twenty-four hours or even get assistance via an instant messaging conversation. The people in charge of customer relations know that we want to shop, maybe purchase, and then leave with a very positive impression of the site. A satisfied customer is a good customer. Good customers remain loyal and recommend you to others.

According to the article, what makes an online shopping site successful? Complete this list.

Notes

1 *customer convenience*

2 _____

3 _____

4 _____

5 _____

2 **Find a word in the text that means the same as:**

1 profitable _____ 5 absolutely necessary _____
2 something of the highest importance _____ 6 help _____
3 easy or helpful to use _____ 7 faithful _____
4 fast and organized _____ 8 suggest _____

Now use words from above to complete the sentences.

a Our customers' satisfaction is our top _____.

b If you need _____, please contact our call centre.

c Good communication skills are _____ in any customer care job.

d And you can pay by credit card, which is very _____ when shopping online.

e We can offer a quicker and more _____ level of service with our new call centre.

f If you are happy with our products, please _____ us to a friend.

3 **You are in a meeting with a possible new customer. Answer their questions.**

Q What makes your company different?
A We are very proud of our _____ [1].
We're especially known for our _____ [2].

Q How do you make it easy and convenient for the customer?
A We offer convenience to the customers with _____ [3].

Q How do I get after-sales service?
A We give efficient customer service by _____ [4].

Q What is the most important focus for your customers?
A Our top priority is to _____ [5].

4 **Complete the spidergram on customer service-centred businesses and jobs with words from the list.**

cashier • concierge • hotel • order entry clerk • receptionist • representative • restaurant • sales • shop assistant • teller

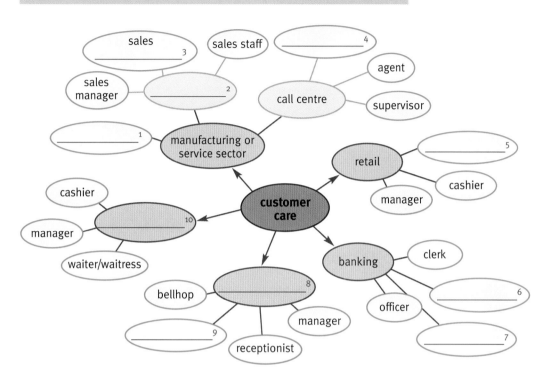

Is your job or business area on the spidergram? If not, add it. Can you add another customer care position?

5 **Now find people in the spidergram that complete the statements below. More than one answer is possible in each case. Compare your answers with a partner.**

1 _____ deals with customers in person.

2 _____ is responsible for helping customers choose the right product.

3 _____ handles customer questions or problems over the phone.

4 _____ takes care of after-sales service.

5 _____ processes product orders for customers.

6 _____ often has to write to customers.

6 Look at the news flash and the extracts from five job advertisements. What kind of 'people' skills do the adverts mention? Complete the notes.

NEWS FLASH

Are technical skills enough?

Customer care is becoming more and more focused on IT training. It's true that nowadays technical skills are essential for working with customer service systems. However, this high-tech training is not enough for good customer care. Employees also need people skills so that they can deal with people in all kinds of customer situations.

Notes

good telephone manner

1 You must be fluent in German and English with a very good telephone manner and good customer service skills. PC skills and good communication skills are required.

2 Customer care and communication skills are essential. Ability to perform effectively under pressure and to work as part of a team.

3 Your role is to provide customers with first-class customer care. Duties: handling telephone enquiries and complaints; making calls to customers; dealing with correspondence by email and letter. Computer skills and good writing skills required.

4 We need someone with the ability to communicate clearly with customers and work effectively with both internal and external teams.

5 You will need experience of communicating face to face with customers, using tact and diplomacy.

What kind of skills do you need for your job? Write a job advert for your position.

7 Here are some comments taken from customer service questionnaires. Mark them *positive* P or *negative* N.

1 'Your sales staff are impatient. They never wait for people to finish speaking and are always in a hurry.' ☐

2 'The people working at your call centre are always so polite and helpful. And they always take the time to answer all my questions.' ☐

3 'I wish your employees would be more attentive. They don't seem to listen to what I say and don't care about me at all.' ☐

4 'The bank officer took care of my requests straight away. I didn't have to wait at all.' ☐

5   'When I arrived at your hotel, I was totally ignored by both the bellhop
    and the receptionist.' ☐
6   'The clerk was really rude and pretended not to see me.' ☐
7   'The waiter was well informed about the the menu and was prompt in bringing my food.' ☐
8   'Your service was more than I asked for. That really made me feel special.' ☐

8   **Complete the table with opposites from exercise 7.**

positive	negative
to be attentive [1]	to ignore somebody
to take the time	[2]
polite	[3]
[4]	uninformed
[5]	too slow
patient	[6]
[7]	unhelpful
[8]	ordinary

Now use words from the table to complete these sentences from a customer care handbook.
Sometimes more than one answer is possible. Compare with a partner.

a   Customers always expect you to be _____ .

b   If you are _____ to customers, they will not do business with you again.

c   Being _____ always makes a bad impression on customers or guests.

d   You should be _____ about the services or products you provide.

e   A call centre agent should never be _____ on the phone and should
    always be _____ .

9   **Tell your partner about one positive and one negative customer care situation you have recently**
    experienced. Make a list of suggestions to improve negative service. Use phrases from the
    Language Box below in your discussion.

USEFUL LANGUAGE	
Making suggestions	**Responding to suggestions**
Why don't you …?	That's right./I agree.
Don't/Wouldn't you agree that …?	I see your point.
Isn't it a better idea to …?	I disagree because …
It makes a good/bad impression if they/you …	I don't agree. I would …

OUTPUT

How much do you know about customer care? Mark the following statements *Agree* [A] or *Disagree* [D]. Then read the article to see how your answers compare.

1 Customers do not tell their friends and colleagues about bad customer care experiences. ☐
2 The product itself is more important than the service behind it. ☐
3 Good, friendly service will keep customers coming back. ☐
4 After the sale is finished, the customer does not need any attention. ☐

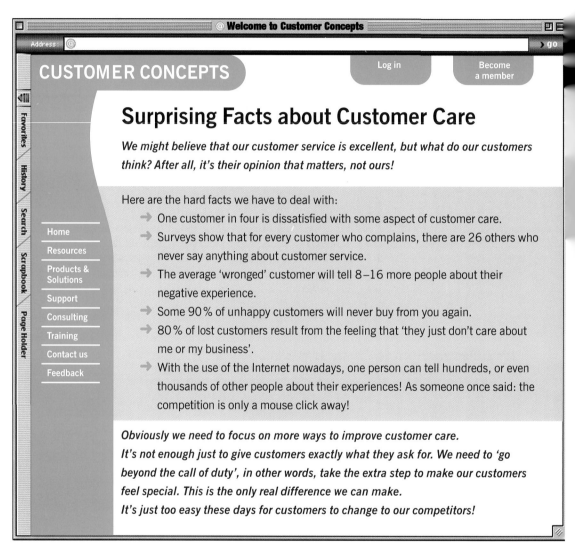

@ **Welcome to Customer Concepts**

Address: @   › go

CUSTOMER CONCEPTS

Log in   Become a member

Favorites | History | Search | Scrapbook | Page Holder

Home
Resources
Products & Solutions
Support
Consulting
Training
Contact us
Feedback

Surprising Facts about Customer Care

We might believe that our customer service is excellent, but what do our customers think? After all, it's their opinion that matters, not ours!

Here are the hard facts we have to deal with:

→ One customer in four is dissatisfied with some aspect of customer care.
→ Surveys show that for every customer who complains, there are 26 others who never say anything about customer service.
→ The average 'wronged' customer will tell 8–16 more people about their negative experience.
→ Some 90% of unhappy customers will never buy from you again.
→ 80% of lost customers result from the feeling that 'they just don't care about me or my business'.
→ With the use of the Internet nowadays, one person can tell hundreds, or even thousands of other people about their experiences! As someone once said: the competition is only a mouse click away!

Obviously we need to focus on more ways to improve customer care.
It's not enough just to give customers exactly what they ask for. We need to 'go beyond the call of duty', in other words, take the extra step to make our customers feel special. This is the only real difference we can make.
It's just too easy these days for customers to change to our competitors!

OVER TO YOU

- If customer care is so important, why do so many businesses not pay enough attention to it?
- Will there be more of a demand for good customer service in the future? Why, or why not?
- How does your company know if it is giving good or bad service?

2

Face to face with customers

What makes the most impact in face-to-face encounters in customer care? Choose the three most important aspects for you and compare your answer with a partner.

> clear speaking voice • good vocabulary • sense of humour • expensive clothes • pleasant body language • good eye contact • accurate grammar • good grooming

1 First read this tip from an American customer care website. Do you agree? Why, or why not?

> **What customers really notice**
> Your body language – the way you stand or sit, what you do with your arms and hands, whether you are smiling or frowning, and so on – tells the real truth to your customers! Your words may be able to hide that you're bored or uninterested, but your body can't. When meeting a customer, make eye contact within 10 seconds. This creates a bond between you and the customer and it shows your interest in real communication. If you don't make eye contact, the customer could think that you aren't interested – or even worse, that you're ignoring them!

Now decide whether the following body language would give a positive P or negative N impression to your customers.

Do you think this impression is the same for people from all cultures?

AUDIO
2–6

2 Listen to five greetings in typical customer care situations and decide where they take place.

☐ a trade fair   ☐ a bank   ☐ a shop   ☐ a company   ☐ a hotel

Now listen again and complete the sentences. Which sentences can be used when you
a) meet someone new b) meet someone you already know c) offer help and d) ask someone
to do something? Write a, b, c or d.

1 Good morning, Ms Richards. _____? ☐

2 Well, if you need help, just _____ . ☐

3 _____ just fill in this form, please, Mr Rodriguez? ☐

4 Hello. _____ I help you? ☐

5 Nice to _____ , Mr Allen. ☐

AUDIO
7

3 Listen to this start and finish of a company visit and complete the sentences. How well does Peter
know his two hosts, Frank and Annie? Has he met them before?

Frank Good morning, you _____[1] Peter Masters. I'm Frank Wepler. Welcome to IGS.

Peter Thank you. It's nice to finally meet you face to face.

Frank Yes, we've talked so much on the phone, I feel I know you already. Peter, I'd like to

_____[2] you to Annie Thomas, our customer services manager. Annie, this is Peter

Masters from TopForm, in Bristol.

Peter Nice to meet you, Ms Thomas.

Annie _____[3] to meet you, too.

Frank So, if you'd just come this way …

Annie _____[4] your flight from Bristol?

Peter It was fine. It even arrived a bit early.

Annie And is this your first time in Brussels?

Peter No, it's my third. I've been here a couple of
times as a tourist. I really like the city.

Frank So, here we are. _____[5] your
coat?

Peter Oh, that's very kind of you.

Frank If _____[6] to take a seat …

Peter Thank you.

Frank _____[7] care for coffee or tea?

Peter Tea would be nice, with two sugars.

■ ■ ■

Peter So, here's my taxi. Well, _____[8] for a good meeting. It was great to meet both of you.

Frank The same for us. Thanks for _____[9]. It was a very productive meeting. So, we'll be
in contact by email as usual.

Peter Yes, of course. Bye.

Annie Have a nice _____[10]! Bye.

Frank So long for now.

Now add phrases from the dialogue to fit the categories below.

Greetings and introductions
Good morning. You must be … . I'm …
_____
_____
_____
_____
_____

Offering hospitality
_____
_____
_____

Saying goodbye
_____
_____
_____
_____
So long for now.

Small talk questions
_____
_____

4 **Complete the sentences with words from the box.**

> care • contact • finally • get • introduce • journey • kind •
> like • long • may • pleasure

1 May I _____ you to Mrs Burton? She's our regional manager.

2 It's nice to _____ meet you face to face.

3 _____ I take your jacket?

4 Oh, that's very _____ of you.

5 I'd _____ to introduce myself. My name's Ralph Lee. I'm the floor manager here.

6 Would you _____ for coffee or tea?

7 Can I _____ you some mineral water?

8 We'll be in _____ by email as usual.

9 It was a _____ to meet you. Have a nice _____.

10 So _____ for now.

CUSTOMER FOCUS EXTRA

Small talk may seem to deal with unimportant topics, but it is necessary for 'breaking the ice' with customers. People can relax and get comfortable with light topics such as:
- their trip (*How was your flight? Did you have any trouble finding us?*)
- where they are staying (*So, how's your hotel? Everything OK?*)
- (first) impressions of the city (*Have you ever been to … ? So, what do you think of … so far?*)
- the weather (*Great weather, isn't it? How's the weather in … ?*)

Be careful with making small talk on topics like family, religion or politics, or with making compliments about somebody's appearance. Depending on your customers' cultural background, they might find the topics too aggressive or too personal in a business context.

5 Match items from the three columns to make mini 'small talk' conversations.

1 So, have you ever been to Vienna before?	a Yes, no problem. It's a very nice location here, isn't it?	A That's good. We've been having a bit of trouble with the trains. They always seem to be late.
2 How was your trip?	b Actually, they're both on holiday now. In Portugal.	B You're lucky. It's been raining here for three days now. Very depressing.
3 Did you find us OK?	c Yes, I have. I was here four years ago.	C Me too. In fact, I'm playing in a tournament this weekend.
4 How was the weather in London?	d Yes, I play in a local club.	D How lovely. I was in Portugal two years ago. Do you know it?
5 So, how are Pat and John doing? Are they still working hard?	e It was fine. The train was a bit late but we arrived on time.	E Oh, really? Was that for business or pleasure?
6 Oh, are you interested in tennis?	f Nice, actually. It was sunny and warm when I left.	F Yes, we like it. We've been here for four years now.

6 Work with a partner to practise meeting a customer for the first time. Use the flow chart below or make a dialogue that fits your own situation.

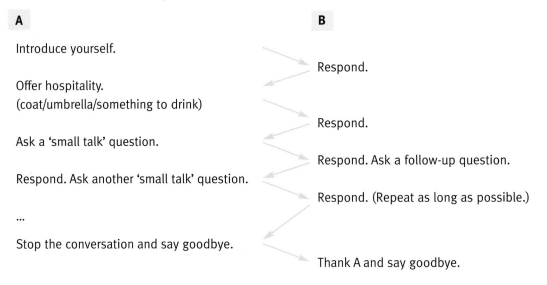

A

Introduce yourself.

Offer hospitality.
(coat/umbrella/something to drink)

Ask a 'small talk' question.

Respond. Ask another 'small talk' question.

...

Stop the conversation and say goodbye.

B

Respond.

Respond.

Respond. Ask a follow-up question.

Respond. (Repeat as long as possible.)

Thank A and say goodbye.

CUSTOMER FOCUS EXTRA

Good basic socializing skills help build your customer base. From the beginning, your customers will see how you show interest and pay attention. This is an important step in establishing a rapport with your customers.

7   **Look at the text from a customer care manual and fill in the missing *do's* and *don'ts*.**

Meetings are an important tool for building your customer base. They provide a great opportunity to network with your customers for future business. Look at these do's and don'ts for successful customer meetings.

- *Do*_____ prepare for your meeting.
- *Do*_____ make sure you know about all your products or services.
- *Don't*_____ take control of the discussion. _____ let the customers decide what they talk about and when they talk about it.
- _____ give customers only the information they want. _____ overwhelm them with extra information that they don't really need.
- _____ use jargon or words only people in your company or industry know.
- _____ talk more than your customers. _____ listen carefully to what they say and _____ interrupt them.
- _____ ask for feedback and clarification, so you'll know exactly what your customers want and need.
- _____ be open, honest, flexible, and positive!

We know exactly what you want. ✗

What we need is... ✓

Can you add any other helpful tips based on your meetings with customers?

8   **Look at these pairs of sentences. Which one would be more effective in a meeting? Refer to the do's and don'ts in exercise 7.**

1   a   OK, let's get started. Unfortunately, I've got another appointment in an hour.
    b   Thanks for coming today. I'm glad to help you review your business needs.

2   a   As I understand it, you'd like to discuss …
    b   This is what we're going to talk about …

3   a   So, that was my suggestion. Is that suitable for you? I'd like to get your feedback.
    b   So, that's the right service for you. I don't think we need to discuss this any more.

4   a   OK, we'd better stop now. I really must go to my next meeting.
    b   Let's go over our action points once more. I want to be sure we agree.

5   a   I've done some research into your company. It seems you …. Is that right?
    b   So, can you tell me something about your company?

6   a   I don't think we can do that. We never offer that kind of discount.
    b   I'll see what I can do.

9 Work with a partner. Use the information in the Partner Files (or make up your own) to role-play a meeting from first greetings to goodbyes.

PARTNER FILES ▶ Partner A File 1, p. 58
Partner B File 1, p. 60

AUDIO
8

10 Listen to a conversation at a trade fair between a sales rep and a potential customer. Mark the statements true ☑ or false ☒, or don't know ❓.

1 Lewis has made an appointment to meet Velleda at the stand. ☐

2 This is Velleda's fifth time at the trade fair. ☐

3 Lewis is interested in a particular product. ☐

4 Velleda gives Lewis a catalogue to take back to his company. ☐

5 Lewis agrees to put his name on the mailing list. ☐

6 Velleda will telephone Lewis in two weeks to set up a follow-up appointment. ☐

Write Velleda's notes about the meeting with Lewis. What does she need to do when he is back in the office?

Accutech

Accutech UK
25 Bridge St
Wisbech, Cambridgeshire
PE13 5JP

Lewis Gillan
Account Manager

Tel +44 1945 579235
Fax +44 1945 579266
email gillan@accutech.uk.com

Notes

_____

_____

_____

_____

_____

AUDIO
8

11 Complete these extracts from the dialogue with words from the box. Then listen again to check your answers.

anything • ask • brochure • email • enjoying • free • glad •
introduce • mind • put

1 May I _____ myself? I'm Velleda Brunelli. I work for Mecro Internazionale in Milan. May I _____ your name?

2 So, Mr Gillan, how are you _____ the trade fair?

3 Well, then, are you looking for _____ in particular?

4 OK, but please feel _____ to ask me any questions. I'd be _____ to go over our products and try to find something suitable for your company.

5   Ah, can I interest you in a _____? It has information about our company and our full range of products.

6   Would you like to _____ your name on our mailing list?

7   Do you _____ if I take your business card? I'll make sure you're on our list. And here's my card. I'll send you a quick _____ next week to see if I can help you with any of our products.

12   **Rewrite the following sentences to make them more polite and effective. Look back at the dialogue for ideas.**

1   Who are you?

2   What are you looking for?

3   Ask me a question if you want.

4   Do you want a brochure?

5   I'll put your name on the mailing list, OK?

6   Give me your business card.

7   I'll contact you sometime soon.

CUSTOMER FOCUS EXTRA

Follow-up is your most important tool for success for any face-to-face encounter. Be sure to be specific about what you will do for your customer, and when you will do it.

Use *I'll* + infinitive to tell the customer of your next action:
   I'll write *you a quick email next week.*
   I'll send *you the latest brochure tomorrow.*
   NOT: ~~I write you …/I send you …~~

Use *would you mind if* + *the past simple*, *do you mind* + *the present simple* or *may* + infinitive (without *to*) to ask if something is acceptable or not.
   Would you mind if I phoned *you on Monday?*
   Do you mind if I ask *you some questions about your company?*
   May I stop by *your office next week?*

Remember, good customer care means taking action to support your words. This builds trust into your customer relationships.

---

13   **Match the questions with the responses.**

1   Would you mind if I put your name on our mailing list?

2   I'll just note that in my diary.

3   Do you mind if I give you my card?

4   I'm afraid I don't have the information here. But I'll call my office and get back to you this afternoon. Is that OK?

5   I'll be in Brixton on Tuesday. Would you mind if I stopped by your office?

6   May I get in touch with you next week?

7   I'll fax you the new price list tomorrow.

a   Tuesday? Yes, that sounds fine. I'll email you directions when I'm back in the office.

b   No, not at all. You can find all my contact information on my card.

c   Sure. I'll look for your phone call on Monday.

d   Yes, that sounds good. I'll stop by the stand at around three.

e   Thanks. That's very kind of you.

f   I'll write it down too. So, we said Monday at 10.30, right?

g   No, let me give you mine, too.

14 Work with a partner. First look at the Useful Phrases below. Then use the information in the Partner Files (or make up your own) to role-play a conversation at a trade fair.

PARTNER FILES ➤ Partner A   File 2, p. 58
Partner B   File 2, p. 60

USEFUL PHRASES

Rep	**Customer**
Could/May I help you?	No, thanks. I'm just looking/browsing.
How can I help you?	I'm looking for/interested in …
May I introduce myself?	My name's …
Could I ask your name?	Nice/Pleased to meet you.
Please feel free to ask me any questions.	Thank you.
Could I offer you/interest you in …?	No, not at all. Let me give you my
Would you mind if I phoned/emailed you?	card/address/number.
It was nice to meet you.	Nice to meet you, too. I look forward to
I hope you enjoy the fair.	hearing from you.
	Thanks, it was a pleasure. I appreciate your
	help.

AUDIO
9

15 Paula Johnston is giving a presentation at a trade fair. Put a–e in the correct order. Then listen to check your answers.

☐ a 'Before I finish, I'll just go over the highlights of this presentation again. Our product and service line includes … . We stand out from our competitors with our excellent follow-up.'

☐ b 'With our impressive line of products and services, we offer special benefits that you can't find with our competitors. Follow-up is our top priority … '

☐ c 'Thanks for your attention. I look forward to having you as a new customer.'

☐ d 'Hello, I'm Paula Johnston from Delta Systems. I'm here today to let you know about some great offers in customer care support services. I'll be speaking about our extensive range of products for tracking new and existing customers …'

☐ e 'I hope you'll pick up one of our leaflets. Also, if you leave me your contact details, I'll be glad to send you our latest catalogue by the end of the week. And if you would like to order today, I'll make sure you receive our introductory price.'

USEFUL PHRASES

- Be natural in your trade fair talk. Do not use memorized speech.
- Follow up quickly. Do not delay in replying to your customers.
- Your customers will remember *you* more than your product or service!

16 **Look at the steps for giving an effective presentation. Match them to phrases (a–i) below.**

Steps for Winning Customers
with Your Presentations

1 Welcome the audience
2 Introduce the subject and give a brief overview
3 Talk about the main product/service features
4 Explain the unique selling points (USPs)
5 Invite interest in the company (products/services)
6 Give promotional information
7 Offer incentives to try a product
8 Finish the talk
9 Show follow-up

a | Step 2 |
I'd like to give you a short preview of my presentation …
We'd like to introduce/show you our latest …

b [ ]
I'll be glad/pleased to send you … by next Monday.
I'll be in contact/touch with you in two weeks.
I look forward to doing business with you.

c [ ]
We stand out from our competitors because …
Our USPs are …

d [ ]
I'd like to welcome you to …
Thank you for coming today.
My name's …
I work for … and I'm in charge of …

e [ ]
Please feel free to pick up a brochure/ leaflet/free sample.
We've got our promotional information and samples available here.

f [ ]
I'd like to offer a special introductory price/discount if you order today.

g [ ]
Our product range includes …
The special highlights are …

h [ ]
We'd be pleased/glad to have you as a new customer.
We'd welcome the chance to do business with your company.

i [ ]
I'd just like to sum up the main points of today's presentation …
Thank you for your kind attention.

Now follow the steps to prepare a short presentation on one of your company's products or services. Try to use the phrases above in your talk.

Read this article from a customer care research site and discuss the questions which follow.

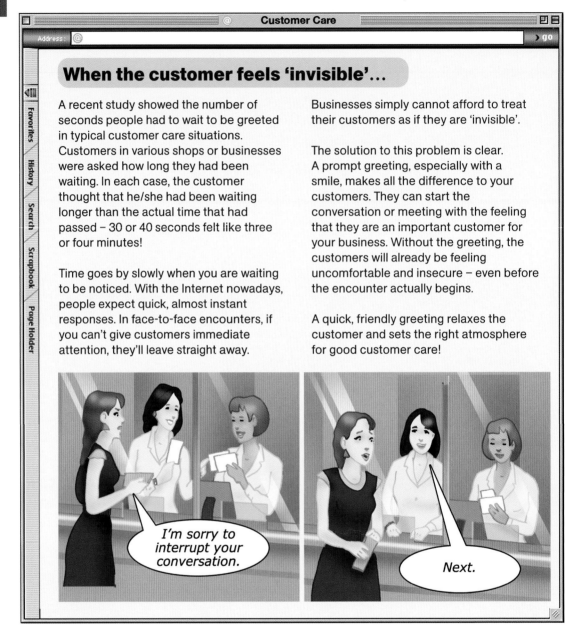

When the customer feels 'invisible'…

A recent study showed the number of seconds people had to wait to be greeted in typical customer care situations. Customers in various shops or businesses were asked how long they had been waiting. In each case, the customer thought that he/she had been waiting longer than the actual time that had passed – 30 or 40 seconds felt like three or four minutes!

Time goes by slowly when you are waiting to be noticed. With the Internet nowadays, people expect quick, almost instant responses. In face-to-face encounters, if you can't give customers immediate attention, they'll leave straight away.

Businesses simply cannot afford to treat their customers as if they are 'invisible'.

The solution to this problem is clear. A prompt greeting, especially with a smile, makes all the difference to your customers. They can start the conversation or meeting with the feeling that they are an important customer for your business. Without the greeting, the customers will already be feeling uncomfortable and insecure – even before the encounter actually begins.

A quick, friendly greeting relaxes the customer and sets the right atmosphere for good customer care!

I'm sorry to interrupt your conversation.

Next.

OVER TO YOU

- Have you ever been ignored – or treated as if you were 'invisible' – in a customer care situation? How did you feel?
- What is the impact on the customer if this happens at a presentation, trade fair, or conference?
- If you are busy with another customer, how can you still notice a customer and make them feel secure and comfortable?

3 Dealing with customers on the phone

How well do you deal with customers on the phone? Answer the questions below for yourself, then compare your answers with a partner.

How often do you ...	always	often	sometimes	never
1 forget the caller's name during a phone call?	☐	☐	☐	☐
2 exchange a bit of small talk with the customer?	☐	☐	☐	☐
3 have to ask the customer to repeat information?	☐	☐	☐	☐
4 forget who you put on hold?	☐	☐	☐	☐
5 take notes during the phone call?	☐	☐	☐	☐
6 have trouble remembering details of the call after you hang up?	☐	☐	☐	☐

1 Listen to two phone calls. What kind of impression do they make? Work with a partner to complete the table.

What went wrong (call 1)	*What went right (call 2)*
_____	_____
_____	_____
_____	_____
_____	_____

Listen to the second call again. How did Martha:

1 answer the phone? *Hello, Martha Greer speaking.* _____ ?

2 say she didn't understand something? *Sorry, could* _____ ?

3 say that there was a mistake? _____ *you've got the wrong extension, Mr Kraft.*

4 offer help? _____ *to connect you?*

5 end the phone call? *I'm putting you through now.* _____ .

CUSTOMER FOCUS EXTRA

Good customer-oriented telephone technique starts with being courteous. This simply means dealing with people in a respectful manner.

CUSTOMER FOCUS EXTRA

Here are some helpful tips for being courteous on the phone.

- Use polite language to show that you really care about the customer and their needs. With *Would you like …?* you ask the same question as with *Do you want …?* but in a more customer-friendly way.
- Use the customer's name throughout the conversation. This makes the customer feel special and helps build rapport.
- Show you are serious about taking care of the customer's requests with your good listening skills and dependable follow-through.
- Finally, do not forget to thank the customer. A simple phrase like *We appreciate your business* or *Thank you for calling* leaves a positive impression at the end of a phone call.

AUDIO

12–13

2 **Listen to two telephone calls between a receptionist and a caller from England. Then complete the conversations.**

Call 1

Receptionist Good morning. Apex Industries. _____

_____ 1

John Yes, this is John Richards from Customer Zone Software. I'd like to speak to Eva Lang, please. Could you put me through to her?

Receptionist Of course, _____ 2, please. … Oh, it seems that her line is engaged. Could you hold a moment? Or _____ 3 to leave a message?

John I'd prefer to hold for just a minute or two.

■ ■ ■

Receptionist Mr Richards? _____ 4. I'm putting you through to Ms Lang's office now. If you get cut off for some reason, please get back to me.

John I'm sorry. Could you speak up a bit? I didn't _____ 5 that.

Receptionist Sure. I'm connecting you now to Ms Lang's office. If you don't get through, please ring again. We're having some problems with our phone system.

Call 2

Receptionist Good morning. Apex Industries.

John This is John Richards again. _____ 6 I got cut off when you tried to put me through.

Receptionist I'm _____ 7 about that.

John I really need to get through to Ms Lang this afternoon. Could I leave a message for her to ring me back as soon as possible?

Receptionist _____ 8, Mr Richards. Could I have your phone number, please?

John	Yes, I'm calling from my mobile. It's 0044 7721 332558.
Receptionist	Right. So, that's 0044 7721 332558. _____ [9] she calls you back today. Could I help you with anything else?
John	Would it be possible to have her mobile number? Could you perhaps look it up for me?
Receptionist	Yes, that's _____ [10]. I've got it right here. It's 49 for Germany, then 156 8877944.
John	Let me just repeat that. That's 49 156 8877944.
Receptionist	That's right.
John	OK. Thanks once again. Bye for now.
Receptionist	You're welcome. Goodbye.

Now write the message that the receptionist takes.

☎ Message

Message for _____

Caller: _____

Company: _____

Message: _____

3 **Match the statements or questions with the responses.**

1 Thank you.
2 I'm afraid he's not in.
3 May I help you?
4 I'll make sure he gets the message straight away.
5 I'm afraid I got cut off.
6 Could I leave him a message?
7 My name is Anton Czrisinski.
8 I'm sorry. Could you spell that, please?

a Thank you. I really appreciate it.
b Yes, certainly. I'll just get a pen.
c You're welcome.
d Yes, I have a question about your price list.
e That's OK. I'll call back later.
f Yes, it's P–F–A– double-F.
g Oh, I'm terribly sorry about that. Let me put you through again.
h I'm sorry. I didn't quite catch that.

CUSTOMER FOCUS EXTRA

If you don't understand the customer, ask him or her politely to say something again or more slowly. You want to be sure you understand so that you can deal with the customer efficiently. Try phrases like:
I'm sorry, but I didn't (quite) catch that/understand you exactly.
Could we go over that once more?
Could you repeat that, please?
Could you speak a bit more slowly, please?
Could you speak up a bit, please?

4   **Complete the sentences with the correct form of phrasal verbs from the box.**

> cut off • get back to • get through to • look up • put through • speak up

1   When I called the hotel, the operator _____ me _____ to the General Manager's office.

2   I'll _____ the address in our directory for you.

3   This is a terrible line. Could you _____ a bit, please?

4   There seems to be something wrong with his extension number. I've tried it three times and got _____.

5   It took a long time, but the customer finally _____ the help desk.

6   I'm sorry, but Ms Allen's in a meeting right now. I'll ask her to _____ you as soon as she's free.

AUDIO 14

5   **Choose the correct words to fit the telephone conversation. Then listen to check your answers.**

Maria   Santos Group, how can I help?

Henry   Hello. Could I have extension 226, please?

Maria   I'm sorry, the line's engaged. Could you please hold/wait ¹? ... Sir, the line's free now. I'll put/pass ² you through.

Henry   Thanks.

Carlos   Service department.

Henry   I'd like to tell/speak ³ to Mr Martinez, please. Is he available at the moment?

Carlos   Will/May ⁴ I ask who's calling?

Henry   Henry Jones. I'm calling from GPT Ltd in London.

Carlos   Just a moment please, Mr Jones. I'll see if he's available. ... Mr Jones? I'm afraid Señor Martinez is in a meeting. Would you like to leave/list ⁵ a message?

Henry   Yes, please ask him to get behind/back to ⁶ me as soon as possible. My number's 44 207 563 361.

Carlos   I'm sorry/afraid ⁷ I didn't catch that. Could you repeat/say ⁸ the number, please?

Henry   Yes, it's 44 for the UK, then 207 563 361.

Carlos   OK, I'm sure/I'll make sure ⁹ he gets the message. Is there anything/anyone ¹⁰ else I can do for you?

Henry   No, thanks.

Carlos   Goodbye, then, Mr Jones. Thanks for calling.

Henry   You're welcome. Goodbye.

6 **Work with a partner to practise a telephone call. Use the flow chart below or make a dialogue that fits your own situation.**

A

Answer the phone.

X is in a meeting. Message?

Respond. Message?

Confirm caller's name. Phone number?

Check message with caller.

Thank the caller and say goodbye.

B

Say who you are and ask to speak to X. (It's urgent.)

Ask when the meeting finishes.

Leave message.

Give your details.

Confirm or correct message.

Say goodbye.

7 **Peter Brenner is a sales rep. Listen to the telephone conversation and complete his notes.**

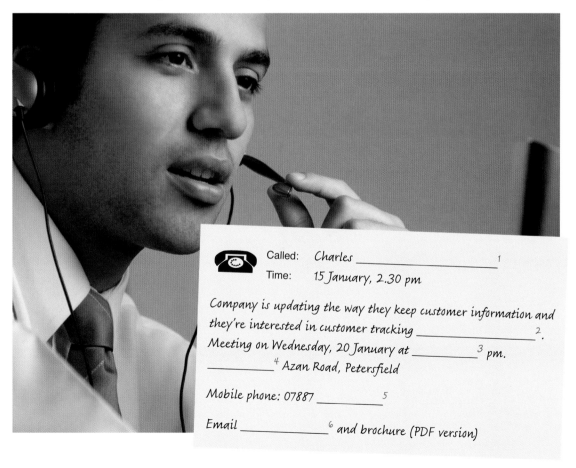

Called: *Charles* _____ *1*
Time: *15 January, 2.30 pm*

Company is updating the way they keep customer information and they're interested in customer tracking _____ *2.*
Meeting on Wednesday, 20 January at _____ *3 pm.*
_____ *4 Azan Road, Petersfield*

Mobile phone: 07887 _____ *5*

Email _____ *6 and brochure (PDF version)*

AUDIO

15

Listen to the dialogue again and tick ☑ the sentences you hear.

1 a Hello, Mr Thomas, I got your contact details from one of my colleagues. ☐
  b Hello, Mr Thomas, I'm responding to your email enquiry. ☐

2 a Would Wednesday suit you? ☐
  b Could we set up a meeting for Wednesday … ? ☐

3 a Could I just confirm that I have the right address? ☐
  b Let me just make sure I have the right address. ☐

4 a Is there anything else I can do for you … ? ☐
  b How else can I help you today? ☐

5 a I look forward to seeing you on Wednesday … . ☐
  b See you on Wednesday at … . ☐

8 **Look at these basic steps for making a successful customer care phone call. Did Peter Brenner follow all the steps in his phone call? If necessary, listen again to check.**

Starting the phone call

1 Identify yourself and your company
2 Say why you are calling

During the phone call

3 Use the customer's name throughout the conversation
4 Take notes of the important information
5 Ask questions to clarify information
6 Repeat and summarize

Finishing the call

7 Tell the customer what you're going to do
8 Make the customer feel confident you'll follow through
9 Offer further assistance
10 Thank the customer

Now say which steps the following sentences go with. Write the appropriate numbers in the boxes. Can you add some other sentences for each step?

Phrases

a ☐ I'm calling to …
b ☐ Could I just go over the details again?
c ☐ Can I help you with anything else?
d ☐ No problem, madam. I'll personally make sure that she calls you back today.
e ☐ I'll just write that down.
f ☐ 1 This is Joan Everts from Everts, Samuels, and Barker.
g ☐ I'll be glad to send this out to you today. You should receive it by …
h ☐ Was that 50,000 or 15,000?
i ☐ Hello, my name is … . I'm with Spectrum PLC in Bristol.
j ☐ I'll check on that information with my colleague and call you back in two hours.
k ☐ I appreciate you taking the time to talk to me.
l ☐ OK, Mrs Armstrong. I'll just …
m ☐ Let me just make a note of that.

9 **Match sentences (1–8) with the more customer-friendly equivalents (a–h).**

1 I'll give you a ring sometime tomorrow.
2 Nice talking to you.
3 Wait, I need to write that down.
4 What's your name?
5 I have no idea, so I really don't know what to tell you.
6 What else do you need? Is that it?
7 I'm putting it in the post today, so you'll probably get it next week.
8 I wrote it down, thanks.

a I'll be glad to send this out to you today. You should receive it by Tuesday.
b One moment, please. I'll just make a note of that.
c Could I take care of anything else for you today?
d May I have your name, please?
e I'll check on that information and call you back in 30 minutes.
f I appreciate you taking the time to call today.
g I'll get back to you at about 11.00 tomorrow morning. Is that OK?
h Let's go over it again to be sure of the details.

10 **Put this phone conversation in the correct order. Then listen to check your answers.**

Susanne Finster

☐ a Nathalie, this is Susanne Finster from Brand AG. We met at the trade fair last week.
☐ b Would Tuesday be convenient for you, at 9 a.m.?
☐ c Bye.
☐ d Hello. May I speak to Nathalie Laurence, please?
☐ e Sounds good. OK, Nathalie, that's Tuesday at 11 o'clock. I look forward to seeing you.
☐ f Fine, thanks. Nathalie, I'm calling to see if we could set up a meeting. You wanted me to do a presentation on our services and I'll be in your area next week.

Nathalie Laurence

☐ g Same here. Thanks for calling. Bye.
1 h Hello.
☐ i Next week? Let me just check my diary. What day exactly?
☐ j Tuesday looks good, but I'm busy at nine. How about 11 o'clock instead?
☐ ⋅k Speaking.
☐ l Ah, yes. Right. How are you?

11 **Match the questions with the responses.**

1 Can we fix a meeting for next Tuesday at nine o'clock?

2 Is Friday the 18th convenient for you?

3 Could we set up a meeting for Thursday afternoon?

4 Are you free next Monday for a meeting?

5 How about one o'clock at my office?

a Monday? Yes, that's fine with me.

b One o'clock is fine with me, but I'd prefer to meet in my office, if that's OK.

c Sorry, I've already got a meeting that morning. How about 1.30 instead?

d I'm off for a long weekend on that date. Can I ring you when I get back?

e Yes, that sounds good. Is two o'clock OK?

12 **Work with a partner to make two phone calls. Study the Useful Phrases below, then look at your role card information in the Partner Files.**

PARTNER FILES Partner A File 3, p. 58 Partner B File 3, p. 60

USEFUL PHRASES

Arranging an appointment
Could we set up a meeting?
Are you available/free on Monday?
Does next Thursday suit you?
How about 2 p.m. on Tuesday?

Agreeing on a time
Just let me check my diary/planner.
Yes, Tuesday is fine with me.
Sounds good. Tuesday at 2 p.m. then.

Suggesting a new time
I'm sorry, but I've got another engagement.
How about Tuesday morning instead?
Actually, Thursday morning would work out better for me.

Confirming
We'll see each other next Thursday at 11.00 at your office.
Could you confirm the details in an email?
Here is my mobile number in case you need to reach me.
I look forward to seeing you.

13 **Use the clues to complete the puzzle and find the hidden word (something one should always try to be when dealing with customers).**

1 IFNCROM: *I'm calling to … our appointment.*

2 *Thanks for … . I can put you through now.*

3 *Could we … a meeting for 3 p.m.?* (2 words – 3, 2)

4 *Thanks for calling. We … your business.*

5 *I'm sorry. I didn't quite … what you said. Could you repeat it, please?*

6 *Would Monday morning be … for you? Perhaps at 9.30?*

7 *Could we go over that … more?*

8 *… care to leave a message?* (2 words – 5, 3)

9 *Can you give me her … number, please?*

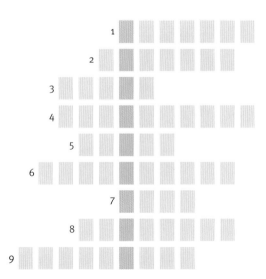

UT

Read this article from a customer care online magazine and answer the questions which follow.

Customer Care *Insight Newsline*

| Quick links ⬍ | Login: User [   ] | Password [   ] | How to join |

| *Search the site* | Home | About us | Membership | Information centre | Shop | Contact us |
| [   ] Go | ☞ | ☞ | ☞ | ☞ | ☞ | ☞ |

What the customers really hear ...

Customer care experts remind us to be careful of 'background noise' while dealing with customers on the phone. The phone receiver picks up even the slightest movement or noise. Keep these 'noise' awareness tips in mind:

- Don't try to talk to someone in your office while you're on the phone. The customer needs your full attention.
- Be sure to put the customer on hold if you're going to discuss something with a colleague. (Remember, always ask first before putting someone on hold.)
- Don't drink or eat during a call. The customer can hear you sipping and chewing.
- Don't smoke while talking to the customer. The customer can also hear you inhale and exhale.
- When you complete the call, hang up the phone gently. If you slam down the receiver, the customer might hear it and think you are annoyed or angry.

All these situations can give the customer the wrong message: I don't care about the customer. This can be quite embarrassing. It may even lead to the customer walking away from your business – never to return!

It's that Mrs Smith again!

OVER TO YOU

- Describe your own work atmosphere. What kind of 'noise' could cause a problem during your customer calls? How can you remove these distractions?
- Share a personal story of when you heard 'background noise' on the phone to a customer services department. What kind of impression did the business make on you?

Call centre success

A survey was carried out recently on call centres for various industries in the UK.
Work with a partner to select the correct answers in these survey results.
Then check the key on page 64 for the answers. Were there any surprises?

1	12% 24% 42% of calls were rated unsatisfactory.
2	Agents were rude in 11% 21% 31% of calls.
3	9% 16% 25% of calls were answered after more than 30 rings.
4	In 7% 10% 14% of calls, agents didn't have enough knowledge to handle the call.
5	In 32% 46% 62% of calls, agents didn't spend enough time understanding the caller's actual needs.

Would a survey in your country have similar results? Why, or why not? How could call centres
change the way customers rate them?

AUDIO
17–18

1 Listen to two call centre conversations. Which customer is placing an order and which has asked
for help?

Listen again and complete the table.

	Call 1	Call 2
Customer		
Customer interested in		
Follow-up		

2 **Complete these sentences from the dialogues. Listen again if necessary.**

Call **1**

1 _____ that you need some assistance.

2 _____ type this in ... one moment ... OK.

3 As _____ it, the problem begins with entering the password. _____ ?

4 I _____ the service technicians' schedule and I _____ back in half an hour.

5 Does that sound _____ ?

6 _____ you with anything else today?

Call **2**

7 One moment, _____ your customer file on my screen.

8 So, Mr Walker, what can I _____ you?

9 I _____ your order as urgent so that the items will be sent out _____ .

10 _____ for your order. Goodbye.

CUSTOMER FOCUS EXTRA

In any call centre situation, the first impression is crucial. Customers will remember how you treated them during the first contact and it may be the only chance to show that you are willing to satisfy the customer. When customers notice professionalism and customer-focus from the very beginning, their perception of the company is a positive one. If not, their impression is negative – and usually stays that way!

Follow these tips for making a good impression:
1 Use your voice and polite language to signal a friendly 'ready-to-help' attitude.
   Gerry speaking. How can I help you today?
   What can I do for you?
   Is there anything else I can help you with today?
2 Listen carefully and make sure you understand your customers.
   I see. So, as I understand it, ... Is that correct?
   Let me just repeat that.
3 Make sure your customer understands you and is happy with the service.
   Does that sound all right?
   Do you have any other questions?
   I hope this is to your satisfaction.
4 Make promises and keep them.
   Your order will go out overnight today.
   I'll call you back in half an hour.
5 Always follow up and follow through.
   I'll ring you when the technician has finished the repair work to make sure everything is all right.

---

3 **Match the two parts to make sentences and questions.**

1 How can I
2 I will personally make sure
3 I hope this is
4 Could you give me
5 Does that sound
6 Is there anything else
7 I'll take care
8 Let me just

a all right?
b of this straight away.
c help you?
d to your satisfaction.
e repeat that.
f that you receive the information this afternoon.
g I can assist you with today?
h your account number, please?

AUDIO
19

4   **Complete the call centre dialogue with the phrases below. Then listen to check your answers.**

could I go over your order again?

I'd just like to confirm your contact details.

Can I help you with anything else?

May I help you?

Is that right?

Could you give me your customer number, please?

OK, let me just repeat that.

Agent	Good morning. Ace Beverages Helpline. _____ ¹
Customer	Yes, please. I need to place an order for ten more cases of my standard house wine – six red and four white – for my restaurant.
Agent	It sounds like you have ordered from us before. _____ _____ ²
Customer	Of course, here it is … uh … 55008-22.
Agent	Ah yes, Mr Green from Suavo Restaurant. _____ _____ ³ So, that's 91 Walton Street, Reading.
Customer	No, that's our old address. We've just moved to 43 High Street. The new postcode is RG1 2XL.
Agent	_____ ⁴ That's High Street, Reading, RG1 2XL. _____ ⁵
Customer	Yes, that's right.
Agent	OK, I've updated our database. Let me just type in the order … OK …
Customer	Look, I'm really in a bind. Could you do a rush order on the wine so that we get it by this evening?
Agent	Sure, that's no problem. We can dispatch it by 11 o'clock. OK, Mr Green, _____ _____ ⁶. You'd like your standard order of house wine, six cases red, four white. And we'll rush the order so that it arrives by approximately 5 p.m.
Customer	Yes, that's all correct. Thank you for helping me so quickly.
Agent	My pleasure. _____ ⁷
Customer	No, thank you. That's all for today. Bye now.
Agent	Goodbye.

5 **Complete the sentences with words from the list.**

> catalogue • dispatched • give • invoice • overnight •
> payment • place • quote • rush

1 Are you ready to _____ your order today?
2 Are you planning to pay by transfer or credit card, or would you like to have a monthly
   _____ plan?
3 OK, sir, the goods are in stock and can be _____ straight away.
4 If it's urgent, we can send it as a _____ order to make sure you receive it by
   Thursday. Would you prefer that?
5 Can you _____ me the item number from the _____, please?
6 Let me check and call you back in one hour with a _____ on the price.
7 We'll enclose the _____ with the goods.
8 We can send the goods by _____ delivery so that you'll get them the next day.

6 **Look at the dialogue. How would you improve the agent's language to make a good impression on the customer?**

Customer	Hello. John Norman speaking.
Agent	Please speak up. I can't understand your name. [1]
Customer	I said, this is John Norman. That's N-O-R-M-A-N.
Agent	Thanks, Mr Norman. Need some help today? [2]
Customer	I'd like to have the latest accountancy software.
Agent	The latest what? [3]
Customer	The latest accountancy software package you've got in your catalogue.
Agent	OK, how many packages do you want? [4]
Customer	I'd like five, please.
Agent	Good. Now I need your address. [5]
Customer	234 Delman Road, Brighton BN1 4QJ, England.
Agent	Fine. I've got that. Anything else? [6]
Customer	Well, when will I receive the software?
Agent	Maybe sometime next week. I've got another call coming in, so bye for now! [7]

Write customer-focused sentences to replace 1–7 above.

1 _____

2 _____

3 _____

4 _____

5 _____

6 _____

7 _____

AUDIO
20

7 Listen to this telephone conversation from a customer to a helpline. Choose the correct answers to complete the sentences.

1 The customer's MP3 player is
   a an i-go maxi.
   b an i-go mini.

2 He has ... tried to install the software.
   a already
   b not yet

3 The customer first needs to find out
   a what his password is.
   b what operating system his computer has.

4 The customer needs
   a to buy another version of the i-go.
   b to upgrade his system before he installs the software.

5 If the customer registers with the company, he gets ... of free service.
   a two years
   b three years

AUDIO
20

Listen again and tick ☑ the sentences you hear.

1 So, what exactly is the problem? ☐

2 Could you explain the problem in more detail? ☐

3 Could you explain what you've done so far? ☐

4 That means you need to have ... ☐

5 In other words, you need to have ... ☐

6 Do you have any questions so far? ☐

7 Are you following me all right? ☐

8 Is everything clear up to now? ☐

9 Are you having any trouble seeing that? ☐

10 Let me just talk you through the steps. ☐

11 This is what I'm going to do. ☐

12 By the way, have you registered with us? ☐

USEFUL PHRASES

Clarifying and explaining
What do you mean exactly?
Sorry, what does that mean?
What exactly does OS stand for?
We just need to clarify a few things.
Could you explain what you've done so far?
Is that X or Y?
That means you need to ...
In other words, you have to ...
That's another word for X.

Checking comprehension
Can you find/see that all right?
Are you having any problems/trouble finding/seeing that?
Are you following me all right?
Is everything clear so far/up to this point?
Do you have any (other) questions so far/up to this point?

8   **Put the words in the right order to make typical 'call centre' sentences. In each sentence there is one word that you do not need.**

1   just   things   need   clarify   a   we   few   to   must   .

_____

2   anything   so   far   clear   everything   is   ?

_____

3   far   you   done   tell   what   could   you've   explain   so   ?

_____

4   that   to   some   means   software   you   need   mean   install   .

_____

5   does   OS   what   for   do   stand   ?

_____

6   what   do   this   I'm   to   when   going   is   .

_____

7   me   you   just   steps   talk   through   the   let   us   .

_____

CUSTOMER FOCUS EXTRA

Use 'signal' sounds and phrases to show you are listening carefully. It is important that the customer knows you are at the other end of the line and listening closely to what they are saying.

Use these phrases or words to show that you …
- are following what the customer is saying: *Uh uh./I see./Right./OK.*
- acknowledge the problem: *Really?/Is that so?/Oh, dear. (BrE)*
- agree: *Uh uh./Of course.*
- are surprised: *You don't say! (AmE)/Really?*

---

9   **Complete these extracts from call centre dialogues with a 'signal' word or phrase. (C = customer / A = agent). Then listen to check your answers.**

C   I left a message for the call centre manager to call me back. That was three days ago and I've heard nothing from him.

A   _____[1] I'm so sorry. Let me see if I can help you …

C   I've emailed your helpline three times, but the emails have all been returned.

A   _____[2] I'm sorry about that. We must have had a problem with our server. It seems to be working all right now though. How can I help you?

C   I'm having trouble with my television. It turns on and I can see the picture, but I can't seem to get any sound.

A   _____[3]. OK, I'm going to need to ask you some questions …

C   Your product is very good, but I'd like more information on an upgraded model.

A   _____[4]. I think I can suggest something for you …

10   **Choose the best response to these call centre questions and requests.**

1   Can't you give me a better price for our first order?
   a   Sorry, I can't do that.
   b   Let me check with the manager and call you back in a few minutes.
   c   It might be possible.

2   Can you quote me a price?
   a   The price is a fair one.
   b   They cost 40 cents each.
   c   Our price is better than our competitors.

3   We are thinking of signing up for your service.
   a   Then why don't you take advantage of our introductory offer?
   b   Call us back when you've decided.
   c   I told you our prices yesterday.

4   Can you do a rush order for me?
   a   I'll try.
   b   Of course. This will go out by the end of the day.
   c   We can't process orders in a hurry, sorry

5   I'd like to order five cases, please.
   a   OK, that's five cases.
   b   Are you sure you only want five?
   c   We have a special offer today: you get one case free when you order six.

6   When can the order be dispatched?
   a   Today, sir, in the overnight post.
   b   Maybe this evening.
   c   I'm not sure. We're having problems with our deliveries at the moment.

11   **Complete the puzzle with the noun form of the verbs.**

Across
1   clarify
5   satisfy
6   explain
8   deliver

Down
2   assist
3   pay
4   offer
7   order

Now complete the sentences with words from the puzzle.

a   Good. I'm glad I could help. Let me know if I can be of any more _____ .

b   I'll put you through to our IT specialist. She'll be able to give you a more detailed _____ and help solve the problem.

c   One of the best things about our introductory _____ is that you can take advantage of our new monthly _____ plan.

12   **Work with a partner to do a 'call centre' role-play. Either refer to the role cards in the Partner Files or think of your own situation.**

PARTNER FILES   Partner A   File 4, p. 58
              Partner B   File 4, p. 60

Read this article from a customer care website and answer the questions which follow.

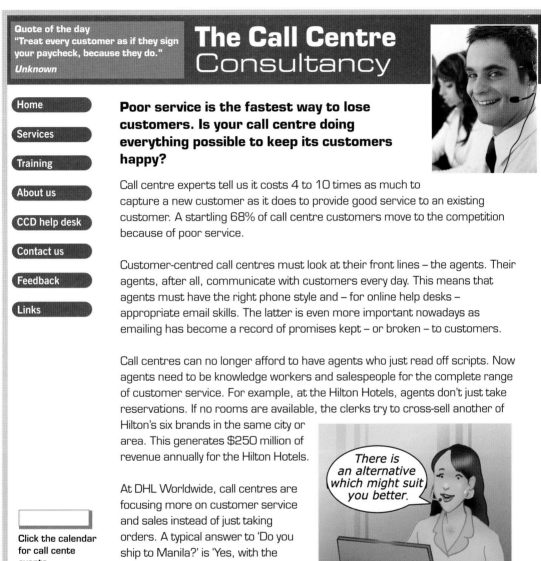

Quote of the day
"Treat every customer as if they sign your paycheck, because they do."
Unknown

The Call Centre
Consultancy

- Home
- Services
- Training
- About us
- CCD help desk
- Contact us
- Feedback
- Links

Poor service is the fastest way to lose customers. Is your call centre doing everything possible to keep its customers happy?

Call centre experts tell us it costs 4 to 10 times as much to capture a new customer as it does to provide good service to an existing customer. A startling 68% of call centre customers move to the competition because of poor service.

Customer-centred call centres must look at their front lines – the agents. Their agents, after all, communicate with customers every day. This means that agents must have the right phone style and – for online help desks – appropriate email skills. The latter is even more important nowadays as emailing has become a record of promises kept – or broken – to customers.

Call centres can no longer afford to have agents who just read off scripts. Now agents need to be knowledge workers and salespeople for the complete range of customer service. For example, at the Hilton Hotels, agents don't just take reservations. If no rooms are available, the clerks try to cross-sell another of Hilton's six brands in the same city or area. This generates $250 million of revenue annually for the Hilton Hotels.

At DHL Worldwide, call centres are focusing more on customer service and sales instead of just taking orders. A typical answer to 'Do you ship to Manila?' is 'Yes, with the fastest delivery time. 99% guaranteed.' Call centre supervisors are now concerned with how well their agents sell DHL, not how quickly they get on and off the phone with customers.

There is an alternative which might suit you better.

Click the calendar for call cente events

Free Newsletter
Register now!
Click here

OVER TO YOU

- Does your company have a call centre? If so, how can your call centre be more customer-centred?
- How can companies motivate their call centre agents to deliver more to their customers?

5

Delivering customer care through writing

Do this quick quiz about writing for customer care. Say whether the statements are true (T) or false (F). Then compare your answers with a partner.

1 The content of a letter or an email is more important than correct spelling and punctuation.

2 It's always better to send an email than to phone a customer.

3 You should always write to new customers in a formal style.

4 If you can understand what you wrote in a letter, then your customer can too.

5 If you have a spellchecker on your computer, you don't need to re-read letters or emails before sending them.

6 Emails should normally be short and concise.

7 If a customer's email or letter is informal, then your reply should also be informal.

8 It's OK to send out standard letters to any customer enquiry.

9 Customers appreciate smileys and other fun graphics in emails.

1 Look at these excerpts from customer care letters and emails. Which one is:

1 an invitation?

2 a follow-up to a meeting?

3 a reply to an enquiry?

4 a promise to send something?

5 a request for information?

a

Hello Mr Sutton

In answer to your email, our shop in Stratford is open Mondays to Saturdays from 9 a.m. to 8 p.m. You can reach us by fax on 0763 449 923.

Please feel free to get in touch if you have any more questions.

Regards
Lara Jones

b

Hi Oliver

We're having a small party at the Wilton Hotel this Friday at 7 p.m. We're asking a few of our most important clients to attend and I would be pleased if you could join us. Let me know if you can come …

Best wishes
Jim

c

Dear Mrs Demetrios

Thanks so much for your phone call yesterday. I am pleased to tell you that we can handle your order. Would you like to pay by credit card or bank transfer? Please fill in the attached form and fax it to me. Then I can send it out to you today.

Best regards
Jeannette Donaldson

e

Robert

I got your message this afternoon. Sure, I'll talk to Ruth and email you the price list today. Do you also need our latest brochure?

Take care
Carola

d

Dear Mr Blair

In regard to our meeting yesterday, I would just like to confirm what we agreed. First of all, …

Sincerely yours
Franco Manzetti

Which of the above are from letters and which are from emails? How can you tell?
Which types of letters or emails do you write to your customers in English?

CUSTOMER FOCUS EXTRA

Salutations and closes
When you write to a customer for the first time, it is often best to use a formal style. Then look at how the customer answers. Is the reply formal or informal? From now on, use the same register as your customer. By communicating with the customer in the way he or she prefers, you demonstrate good customer care.

Here is an overview of standard salutations and closes used in letters and emails.

	letter	email
when you don't know the name	Dear Sir or Madam / Dear Sirs Ladies and Gentlemen (AmE) —— Yours faithfully (BrE) Sincerely (yours) (AmE)	Dear Sir or Madam / Dear Sirs Hello —— (Kind / Best) Regards Best wishes
when you know the name	Dear Mr / Ms / Mrs Smith Dear Mr and Mrs Smith Dear Ms Black and Mr Smith —— Yours sincerely (BrE) Sincerely (yours) (AmE)	Dear / Hello Mr / Ms / Mrs Smith Dear / Hello Mr and Mrs Smith Dear / Hello Ms Black and Mr Smith —— (Kind / Best) Regards All the best / Best wishes
when you know the person / people well	Dear John Dear Paul and Mary —— Kind regards (With) best wishes	Dear / Hello / Hi John Hi Paul and Mary —— Best (wishes) / All the best Take care (AmE) / Cheers (BrE)

Note that in the US, the salutation in letters is often followed by a colon (*Dear Mr Brown:*). In the UK there is often no punctuation used here, but sometimes people put commas after both the salutation and the close (*Dear John*, … *Kind regards*, …). Whether there is a comma or not, the first word in letters and emails always starts with a capital letter.

2 Which salutations and closes should you use when writing to the following people?

informal

1 `em@il` → Hugo Jones
   Hi Hugo ... All the best

2 `letter` → Walter Rogers

3 `letter` → Mario Ingram & Janet Browne

formal

4 `letter` → Carol Elan

5 `em@il` → Jeanne & Pascal Duchard

6 `letter` → name unknown

3 Read the letter and answer the questions.

1 How well does Richard know Mr Davis?
2 Where did they meet?
3 What did Mr Davis request?
4 What will happen next?

Horizons International
42 Windsor Street, London N1 4EJ
Tel +44 20 654 372 • Fax +44 20 654 374 • r.bird@horizint.com

---

John Davis
Davis & Chapman Ltd
145 Cheltenham Rd
Bristol BS6 5QZ

Dear Mr Davis

It was a pleasure meeting you recently at the Business Executive Conference. I am delighted to be able to assist you in finding a suitable IT communications system for your company. As requested, I am enclosing our latest catalogue with details and prices.

I would be grateful if we could meet soon. I will phone you on Thursday and hope we can arrange a suitable date and time.

If you have any further questions, please do not hesitate to contact me.

I look forward to welcoming you as a new and valued customer.

Yours sincerely

Richard Bird

Richard Bird
Sales Manager

4 **Match the two parts to make phrases.**

1 I look forward to
2 We are delighted to
3 If you have
4 Thank you
5 It was a pleasure to
6 If you are satisfied
7 I will pay

a for choosing our company
b seeing you next week
c you a visit personally
d any further questions
e speak to you
f have you as a new customer
g with the results

Now use the phrases to complete this email to a new customer.

From: "Vera Knox" **To:** barbara.winston@gmax.co.uk

Subject: telephone service

Dear Mrs Winston

_____[1] on the phone

yesterday. _____

_____[2]. As you requested, here is a summary of our discussion:

• You will receive monthly service for one year.

• _____[3], you

  can renew your contract for as many years as you would like.

• Your service fees will be invoiced monthly.

• Finally, as you are a new customer, we can offer you a 10% introductory discount on your

  rate if you pay before the due date.

As we agreed, _____[4]

next Thursday, 10 September, at 10.30 to show you how to start up the service.

_____[5], please feel

free to contact me. Otherwise, _____

_____[6].

_____[7].

Best wishes

Vera Knox
Sales Manager

5   **Two versions of the same email – one formal and one informal – have been mixed up. Put them back in order.**

Dear Mr Varley
b
_____
_____
_____

Dear Mike
_____
_____
_____

a   In the meantime, if you have any other questions, please don't hesitate to contact me.
I look forward to seeing you next week.

c   I'm glad to tell you that we've found two new customers for you. It'd be great if we could set up a meeting at the end of next week to discuss this. Would you like me to email you the customer information today? You can review it before we meet.

b   In regard to your phone call this morning, I am writing to let you know about the latest developments.

d   Kind regards
J Hargreaves

e   Thanks for your phone call this morning.
Just a quick email to let you know about the latest developments.

f   I am delighted to inform you that we have found two new customers for you. I would appreciate it if we could set up a meeting at the end of next week to discuss this. Would you like me to email you the customer information today? You can review it before we meet.

g   All the best
John

h   In the meantime, let me know if you need any other help.
Looking forward to seeing you next week.

6   **Now find phrases in the two emails to complete the table below.**

FORMAL	INFORMAL
Connecting with the reader In reference to your letter/email of ... _____ 1	Re your letter/email of ... _____ 2
Further to our recent meeting ...	I hope everything is going well.
Reason for writing We are writing to confirm ... _____ 3	I'm just writing to tell you ... I'd like to let you know ... _____ 4
I would like to inform you ...	
Giving good news We are pleased to say ... _____ 5	_____ 6 I'm happy to tell you ...
Requests We would be grateful if we could ... _____ 7	_____ 8 Could you ... ?
Taking action I will phone you/contact you ... We would be delighted/pleased to assist you.	I'll get in touch with/get back to you ... I'd be glad to help out.
Concluding Please feel free to contact me/us if you have any further questions. _____ 9	Let me know if you need anything else. _____ 11
We look forward to hearing from/meeting you soon. _____ 10	Looking forward to your reply/to hearing from you. _____ 12

7   **Complete the sentences from letters and emails with words from the box.**

back • convenience • hearing • just • of • pleased • regard • reply • would

1   In _____ to your phone call, I am sending you the specifications for model XRT32.

2   We would be _____ to assist you with all your financial planning.

3   Thanks for your letter _____ 29 June.

4   I'll get _____ to you as soon as possible.

5   We look forward to _____ from you soon.

6   I _____ be grateful if you could contact me at your earliest _____ .

7   Looking forward to your _____ .

8   I'm _____ writing to let you know the dates of our next open house.

CUSTOMER FOCUS EXTRA

Follow the five Cs of customer care writing to make sure your writing is:

Clear   Keep sentences short and direct, and have well-organized paragraphs.

Complete   Include all the information your customer needs, including reference numbers and contact details.

Concise   Do not waste your reader's time with too much extra information. Remember your customer is also a busy person.

Courteous Use polite language and follow letter-writing conventions.

Correct   Do not distract the reader with mistakes in grammar, punctuation, and spelling. Always re-read your letter or email before sending it.

---

8 First study the tips in the box above and then say what is wrong with this email. Which of the five Cs has the writer ignored? Rewrite the email.

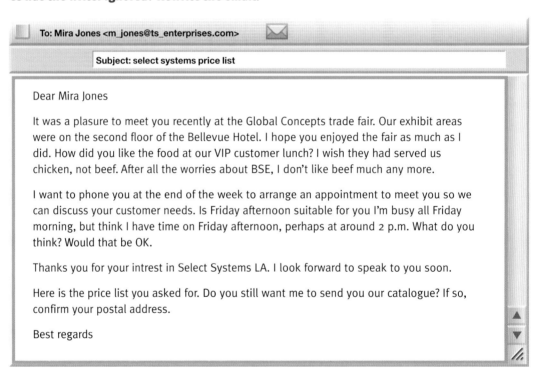

To: Mira Jones <m_jones@ts_enterprises.com>

Subject: select systems price list

Dear Mira Jones

It was a plasure to meet you recently at the Global Concepts trade fair. Our exhibit areas were on the second floor of the Bellevue Hotel. I hope you enjoyed the fair as much as I did. How did you like the food at our VIP customer lunch? I wish they had served us chicken, not beef. After all the worries about BSE, I don't like beef much any more.

I want to phone you at the end of the week to arrange an appointment to meet you so we can discuss your customer needs. Is Friday afternoon suitable for you I'm busy all Friday morning, but think I have time on Friday afternoon, perhaps at around 2 p.m. What do you think? Would that be OK.

Thanks you for your intrest in Select Systems LA. I look forward to speak to you soon.

Here is the price list you asked for. Do you still want me to send you our catalogue? If so, confirm your postal address.

Best regards

AUDIO

22–24

9 Listen to three voicemail messages. Then match them with the written responses below. Which responses are by email and which by letter? How can you tell?

a   ☐ Thank you for your phone call of 2 May. I'm sorry we were not available to take your call.
Please find attached a brochure about our services. You can also visit us online at www.bestfoods.com for more detailed information.
If you have any other questions, please do not hesitate to contact us.

b ☐ Sorry we weren't in when you called.
I've attached a pdf of the specifications for model 830T.
Should I also arrange to send you some product brochures
for the shop?
Let me know if you need anything else.

c

☐ Thank you for your reservation of 2 May.
I'd like to confirm the following:
1 single room with a bath for two nights from 5 to 7 May.
As you requested, we have enclosed a magazine listing all events taking place in May.
Please feel free to contact us if you require any assistance with bookings.
We look forward to welcoming you to our hotel.

CUSTOMER FOCUS EXTRA

Make sure you review your documents carefully before sending them to the customer. Like the letter or email message itself, you need to view it through the customer's eyes. Is it appropriate? Does it present a positive image? Take an extra moment to check the enclosures or attachments before you close the envelope or hit the send button!

You can use the following language to refer to the enclosed or attached documents:

letter	**email**
Please find enclosed/I am enclosing the price list you requested.	*I'm sending you the current price list as an attachment.*
In the enclosed information packet, you will find product descriptions, …	*I've attached the specifications as a pdf document.*
As you will see from the enclosed brochure, …	*Please complete the attached form and return it …*
	Please find attached …
	Here is the file you asked for. (informal)

---

10 **Use the phrases from page 43 and the Language Box above to write a customer-friendly reply to the following email enquiry.**

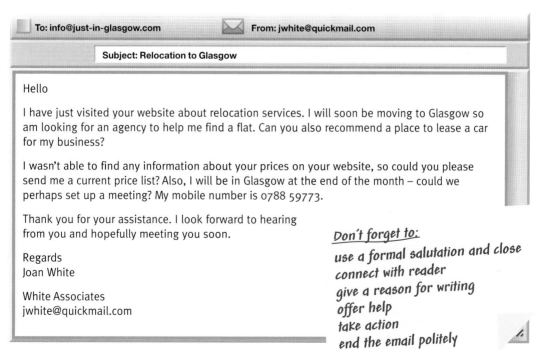

To: info@just-in-glasgow.com   From: jwhite@quickmail.com

Subject: Relocation to Glasgow

Hello

I have just visited your website about relocation services. I will soon be moving to Glasgow so am looking for an agency to help me find a flat. Can you also recommend a place to lease a car for my business?

I wasn't able to find any information about your prices on your website, so could you please send me a current price list? Also, I will be in Glasgow at the end of the month – could we perhaps set up a meeting? My mobile number is 0788 59773.

Thank you for your assistance. I look forward to hearing from you and hopefully meeting you soon.

Regards
Joan White

White Associates
jwhite@quickmail.com

Don't forget to:
use a formal salutation and close
connect with reader
give a reason for writing
offer help
take action
end the email politely

11   **Work with a partner to practise writing emails and letters. Either think of your own situation or look at the ones in the Partner Files. Try to use phrases from this unit.**

PARTNER FILES   Partner A   File 5, p. 59
Partner B   File 5, p. 61

OUTPUT   Read this case study about customer care provided via the Internet and answer the questions which follow.

Giving customers 'the no-answer runaround' –
A CASE STUDY

Customers have become used to the speedy response or quick 'turn-around time' of Internet exchange and are therefore sometimes more demanding and less patient than they used to be. They want quick answers to their service questions. Here is a typical customer experience and its result.

A customer asked a large catalogue store whether a hand-held computer he was planning to buy from their company could be used for PowerPoint presentations. The response was: 'Visit our website under FAQ' (the common abbreviation for 'Frequently Asked Questions'). When the customer looked at the FAQs, he could not find the right question for his problem. His 'search' attempt got no answers either, so he wrote his question in the 'other enquiries' field.

The customer got this answer immediately: 'Thank you for your email. We will try to handle your request as soon as possible. Since we get so many enquiries, it is faster to refer to the FAQ section or use the search tools to find your answer.' The customer was back at the beginning.

...and their website couldn't be more helpful.

The frustrated customer finally gave up and changed to another brand of palm computers. When he emailed the new company's service centre, he got a direct answer with efficiency and courtesy. He was so pleased with the quick and polite service that he recommended the hand-held computer to several of his colleagues.

OVER TO YOU

• Share a personal experience with a partner about dealing with automated online customer care. How did it make a positive or negative impression on you?

• Describe ways a customer service centre can be sure that an automated system gives customers the help they need.

• Does your company have a website offering customer service? If so, how is it set up? What kind of FAQs do you have? How do you deal with enquiries sent via the website?

Dealing with problems and complaints

Look at this list of things that customers complain about. Which three things annoy you the most as a customer? Compare your answers with a partner.

a Being put on hold when you call somebody

f Not enough staff to help customers

b Getting an engaged signal when trying to call

g Receiving too much junk mail or advertising

c Being transferred many times when you call

h Getting complicated, unclear explanations

d Unhelpful staff

e Salespeople with little or no knowledge of their products and services

i Not getting quick answers to emails

Can you add anything else to the list? How can companies avoid annoying their customers?

1 Read this email from a customer service manager to her staff. Work with a partner to write an action checklist for the meeting.

Hello everyone,

Recently we have been getting a lot of complaints from customers who are annoyed with the quality of our customer service. Here are just three of the comments we've received:

'I had a problem with one of your products. When I told the salesperson about it, he was arrogant and acted like my problem was stupid and unimportant. He even suggested that the problem was my fault.'

'The person on the phone didn't even listen to what I was saying. I had to repeat myself two or three times. Then she just said, 'Well, that's our company policy. I can't do anything about it.' She didn't even apologize!'

'I realize I was angry and perhaps spoke sharply, but the agent didn't have to yell at me. He told me it wasn't his fault and that I should speak to the person who made the mistake, not him.'

At our next staff meeting, I want to discuss our complaints policy and how we can improve our customer care. I would like you all to make an action checklist on how to improve the way we handle customers, and present your ideas at the meeting.

2 Here are some of the ideas presented at the meeting. Work with a partner to decide whether they belong to the *do* or *don't* list.

do	don't
_____	_____
_____	_____
_____	_____

1 Let the customers show their anger.
2 Say the problem was the customer's fault.
3 Tell the customer there's nothing you can do.
4 Listen carefully to the details of the problem.
5 Push the customer to accept your point of view.
6 Take the customer's anger as a personal criticism.
7 Offer a more expensive product or service to replace the first order.
8 Summarize and make sure the customer agrees to the plan of action.

AUDIO
25–27

3 Three customers are making complaints. Listen and match the dialogues to the pictures. Then complete the table.

	complaint	response
Dialogue 1		
Dialogue 2		
Dialogue 3		

4 **Listen again and complete these sentences from the dialogues.**

Dialogue 1 1 I'm _____ to _____ that.

2 What _____ to be the _____ ?

3 First of all, _____ for the poor service …

Dialogue 2 4 We've got a lot of people in the same position _____, but don't worry.

5 _____ we'll _____.

6 So, _____.

Dialogue 3 7 It _____ that our shop assistant made a _____.

8 I'll be happy to _____ your money.

9 That's no _____. I'll _____ to help you.

CUSTOMER FOCUS EXTRA

In problems and complaints we often soften bad news by using phrases such as
I'm afraid (that) *we've made a mistake.*
It seems (that) *there has been a mix-up with your order.*
It appears (that) *they forgot to enclose the instructions.*
There seems/appears *to be a misunderstanding.*

We can also combine these phrases with the passive tense to acknowledge the problem without saying who exactly made the mistake.
*It seems/appears (that) the order **was not handled** promptly enough.*
*I'm afraid (that) a mistake **has been made**.*

---

5 **Write a customer-friendly statement for each situation. Use phrases from the Language Box above.**

1 You're wrong. Our information is right, not yours. (seems / misunderstanding)

   There seems to be a misunderstanding.

2 It wasn't my colleague's fault that you didn't get the order. (afraid / mix-up)

   _____

3 The agent didn't put some of the parts in the shipment. (appears / include)

   _____

4 I didn't get your email, so it's obvious that you didn't send it. (seems / get though)

   _____

5 You won't get the order this week. (afraid / delay)

   _____

6 That's a mistake, but it's your fault, not mine. (appears / mistake)

   _____

6 **What is wrong with these answers to a customer's complaint? How do you think the customer would react in each case?**

1 ☐ 'I don't really deal with that. That's not my department.'
2 ☐ 'Well, I've never done that before, but I'll try it and see what happens.'
3 ☐ 'We can't help you with that. We don't carry that product here.'
4 ☐ 'I don't know.'
5 ☐ 'We don't give refunds – as soon as you leave the store, it's yours.'

Look at these more effective answers. Match them with 1–5 above.

a We have an exchange policy, but I'm afraid we don't give refunds. So, please make your selection carefully before buying. Could I help you decide which product is the best for you?

b I could give you some general advice, but it's better if you speak to my colleague. He is the specialist in this area. May I transfer you to him?

c I'm really not certain about that, but I'll find out for you. I'll ring you back by 4 p.m. today. Is that OK?

d I'm afraid this isn't something we carry. I can recommend that you contact T&C. I'm sure that they carry that product.

e That sounds like something we could do for you, but I need to make sure. May I ask my manager about it and call you back?

AUDIO
28

7 **Complete the dialogue about a problem-solving situation in a hotel with phrases from the list. Then listen to check your answers.**

> Excuse me • I can see how • I'd be glad • I'd like to say • inconvenienced • make sure • seems to be • straight away • understand • Would you mind

Guest _____ ¹, I have a complaint about your hotel.

Receptionist Oh, you look very troubled. What _____ ² the problem, madam?

Guest Well, we're regular guests at your hotel, but I'm about to change my mind about ever staying here again! The service is terrible. I've had to ring housekeeping every day to ask them to clean my room. My company pays good rates for me and my colleagues to stay at your hotel, so a dependable cleaning service is the least we expect!

Receptionist First of all, _____ ³ how sorry I am. _____ ⁴ this must have ruined your stay with us. So, if I _____ ⁵ you correctly, you had to phone each day to get your room serviced?

Guest That's right.

Receptionist _____ ⁶ giving me some details? If I could just have your name and your room number and what time you called and who you spoke to exactly …

■ ■ ■

Receptionist   Ms Jones, I'll speak to housekeeping _____⁷. I want to

_____⁸ this never happens again. Since you've been so

_____⁹ by this incident, _____¹⁰ to offer you

two free nights for your next visit at our hotel. In fact, I'll give you a voucher right now.

You can use it any time you wish.

Guest   Oh, that's just great! I am so glad that we could work this out. We do want to keep

coming back here.

8   **How did the hotel receptionist deal with the problem? First complete the statements with the correct form of verbs from the list. Then write down the phrases she used.**

> apologize • ask for • listen • offer • repeat • take

What the receptionist did:	What the receptionist said:
1 She *listened* to the guest carefully.	_____
2 She _____ after hearing the guest's story.	_____
	_____
3 She _____ the problem back to the guest.	_____
	_____
4 She _____ more information about the problem.	_____
	_____
5 She _____ action to help the guest straight away.	_____
	_____
6 She _____ compensation for the guest's trouble.	_____
	_____

CUSTOMER FOCUS EXTRA

We don't want customers complaining over and over again about the same problems. Make sure you ask for as many details as possible to deal with every complaint effectively. Show the customer your intention to take care of the whole problem, not just bits and pieces. This is the key to customer satisfaction for today – and for the future.

9 **Look at the problem-solving flow chart below and match the headings to the steps.**

a Clarify the information and repeat the problem back to the customer.
b End with a friendly, helpful tone.
c Assure the client of follow-up.
d Apologize.
e Summarize the discussion.
f Offer an alternative if the customer doesn't accept the solution.
g Listen carefully to the customer describe the problem and show empathy.
h Say how and when the problem will be solved.
i Take responsibility for the problem.

First of all, I'm so/terribly sorry about that.
I apologize for ...
Let me apologize for ... **1**

Could you tell me exactly what happened?
Could you explain a bit more ... ?
Do you mind if I just go over that again ... ? **2**

I'll just make a few notes as you speak.
I understand./I see what you mean.
I would feel the same way.
What a difficult situation this puts you in. **3**

It looks like an oversight on our part.
There seems to be a misunderstanding.
It appears your order got overlooked.
I'm afraid there has been some sort of mix-up. **4**

I'll take care of this at once for you.
I'm sure we can find a solution.
I'd be glad to offer you ... to make up
   for this inconvenience.
This should be resolved by the end of today. **5**

If this solution does not meet your needs,
   then I can suggest ... as an alternative.
I'll look into other possibilities by ...
I'll get back to you straight away.
You'll receive (a refund/replacement) by
   tomorrow ... **6**

What we have decided is ...
Our action plan is ...
I'd like to go over this once more to make
   sure we agree. **7**

I'll get back to you ...
I'll follow up to make sure that ... **8**

I hope you are satisfied with the outcome.
Thanks for bringing this to our attention.
Is there anything else I can help you with
   today?
Don't hesitate to ring again if there are any
   more problems. **9**

10 Work with a partner. Choose one of the situations below (or think of a situation of your own) and use the information in the Partner Files to do a face-to-face or telephone role-play. Note that Partner A is always the customer. Make sure you follow the steps for problem-solving.

Situation 1 A damaged consignment and a mistake on an invoice
Situation 2 A noisy hotel room on a business trip

PARTNER FILES ▶ Partner A File 6, p. 59
Partner B File 6, p. 61

11 Read this typical letter of apology and complete it with the phrases below.

> We very much regret

> We are very concerned to hear

> Once again, we apologize

> We assure you that we are doing everything we can

> The problem has now been resolved

Dear Mr Webber

_____ [1] that your order from last month
has not reached you. _____ [2] the
frustration this has caused you.

_____ [3] to make sure your
order arrives as soon as possible. The delay was due to an unexpected computer
problem in the delivery department which interrupted our usual efficient service.
_____ [4] and your order
has been sent to you by overnight post.

_____ [5] for the inconvenience. We do
value your business and hope to keep you as a long-term customer.

Yours sincerely

Mark Beckham

Dispatch Manager

Find phrases in the letter above which Mark Beckham used to:

a state the problem
b apologize to the customer
c show empathy with the customer

d explain the reason for the problem
e offer a solution

12 **We sometimes have to explain our company policy when responding to complaints.**
Match the policy with a customer-friendly explanation.

policy

1 ☐ We don't give estimates out on the phone.
2 ☐ We don't ship by regular post, only by overnight express.
3 ☐ We don't send out our diet products unless the customer has been checked by a doctor.
4 ☐ We block any credit card charge that looks unusual or has a high amount.
5 ☐ We can't do anything about our bank service charges.

explanation

a This ensures the safe use of our products.
b We aim to give the highest standards in managing your bank accounts.
c This helps us give you a fairer and more accurate quote.
d This ensures that your food products arrive fresh.
e This is a security precaution to make sure your card has not been stolen.

Can you add another example of your own company policy?
How can you say it in a polite, positive way so that the customer understands and accepts it?

13 **Work with a partner. You both work for Dalton Communications and have received the following**
three complaints. First discuss how to deal with them: by telephone, in person, or in writing.
Then choose one complaint and decide how to respond.

1

I'm writing to you because I've been trying to get through to your helpline for the past three days. I've called several times during the day and night, but have never got through, not even once! I'm trying to enquire about something on my monthly bill. It's useless to have a helpline if it is always busy! I plan to visit your manager next week to discuss this in person.

2

I became a subscriber to your service because you promised six months of cheap phone calls to the UK, which is where my brother lives right now. When I got your invoice though, I was completely shocked to see that the UK phone calls are twice as expensive as before, with my old phone service. What happened to the low, low rates?! I find this misleading advertising totally unacceptable.

3

As a regular customer of yours for nearly five years now, I find this latest incident with your call centre totally unacceptable. I phoned in recently to enquire about the latest service upgrades. The agent informed me that I could not add any other features to my IT system. I only bought the system from you six months ago. The agent told me someone had sold me a 'limited system', so no action could be taken. Then, I asked to speak to her supervisor, so she put me on hold. To my dismay, I got disconnected. I tried to ring back, but again got an engaged signal.

PUT

**Look at what these people say about customer complaints and apologies.
Do any of the comments sound familiar?**

I lived in England for a while and was impressed with how easily the words 'I'm sorry' can help defuse a difficult situation. A lot of my colleagues in my country prefer not to say it when dealing with complaints because they say: 'The problem's not my fault, why should I apologize?' But I just think it means: 'I'm sorry about the situation and want to help you'. It doesn't mean that I'm responsible.

We get a lot of complaints online to our website and it's amazing how rude and insulting some customers can be. Perhaps it's because they think they're not talking to a real person, just a machine. But real people like me read the messages and then have to answer in a friendly and professional manner. Sometimes it's quite difficult to do so and I wonder what these customers would think if I wrote the same type of angry messages to them!

I'm a Canadian living in Europe and I must admit it's taken me a long time to get used to customer service here. I used to be very polite when I complained about a product or service in a shop, for example. I said 'please' and smiled a lot, and the shop assistants just looked at me like I was crazy! I don't think they took me seriously. Now when I have a complaint, I don't smile. I'm very direct and just state my problem. And I get a much better response from the shop assistants this way. Perhaps it's just a cultural thing.

OVER TO YOU

- How do you deal with complaints at your company or business? Is it the same or different from other companies you know or do business with?
- How do people in similar jobs in other countries deal with complaints? Do you think there are cultural differences in the way customers complain and what they complain about? How about the way apologies are made?

Test yourself!

See how much you have learned about customer care. Use the clues to complete the crossword puzzle.

Across

3   Another word for *to seem*: *It ... that we made a mistake.*
4   It's always important to show good listening skills or to be ... to customers.
6   *Sorry, I didn't quite ... that. Could you say it again?*
8   Another way to say *I handle customer orders*: *I'm ... for customer orders.*
9   Another way to say *to phone* or *to call*: *Can I ... you back tomorrow?*
16 A way to offer further assistance: *Can I help you with ... today?* (2 words – 8, 4)
19 Another word for *help*: *How can I ... you?*
20 Another word for *pleased*: *I'd be ... to have you as a new customer.*
21 *I'm ... that we can't send out the software today.*
22 *I'll ... she calls you back today.* (2 words – 4, 4)
24 FOMCRIN: *I'd like to ... your address.*
25 *May I ... that once again to check?* (2 words – 2, 4)
26 *I look ... to hearing from you.*
27 *If you have any questions, please don't ... to contact me.*

Down

1   A way to end a phone call: *Thank you. We ... your business.*
2   Something you want to build or establish with customers: *a good ...*
5   Showing ... means you understand what the customer is feeling.
6   When you want to set up a meeting, you might say: *Would Tuesday be ... for you?*
7   A customer at a trade fair who doesn't want help might say: *No, thank you. I'm just ... .*
10 Another way to say *immediately*: *I'll send you the package ... .* (2 words – 8, 4)
11 YFAIRLC: *We just need to ... a few things.*
12 A way to check that the customer is happy with your service: *I hope this is to your ... .*
13 A way to start a presentation at a trade fair: *I'd like to ... you here today.*
14 Another phrase to say *I'm sorry*: *I'd like to ... for the delay.*
15 When you meet someone for the first time, you can say: *I'd like to ... myself.*
17 We often start a meeting or phone call with ... to make customers feel comfortable. (2 words – 5, 4)
18 To see if something is OK, you can say: *Would you ... if I phoned you tomorrow?*
23 A formal close in email writing: *Kind ...*

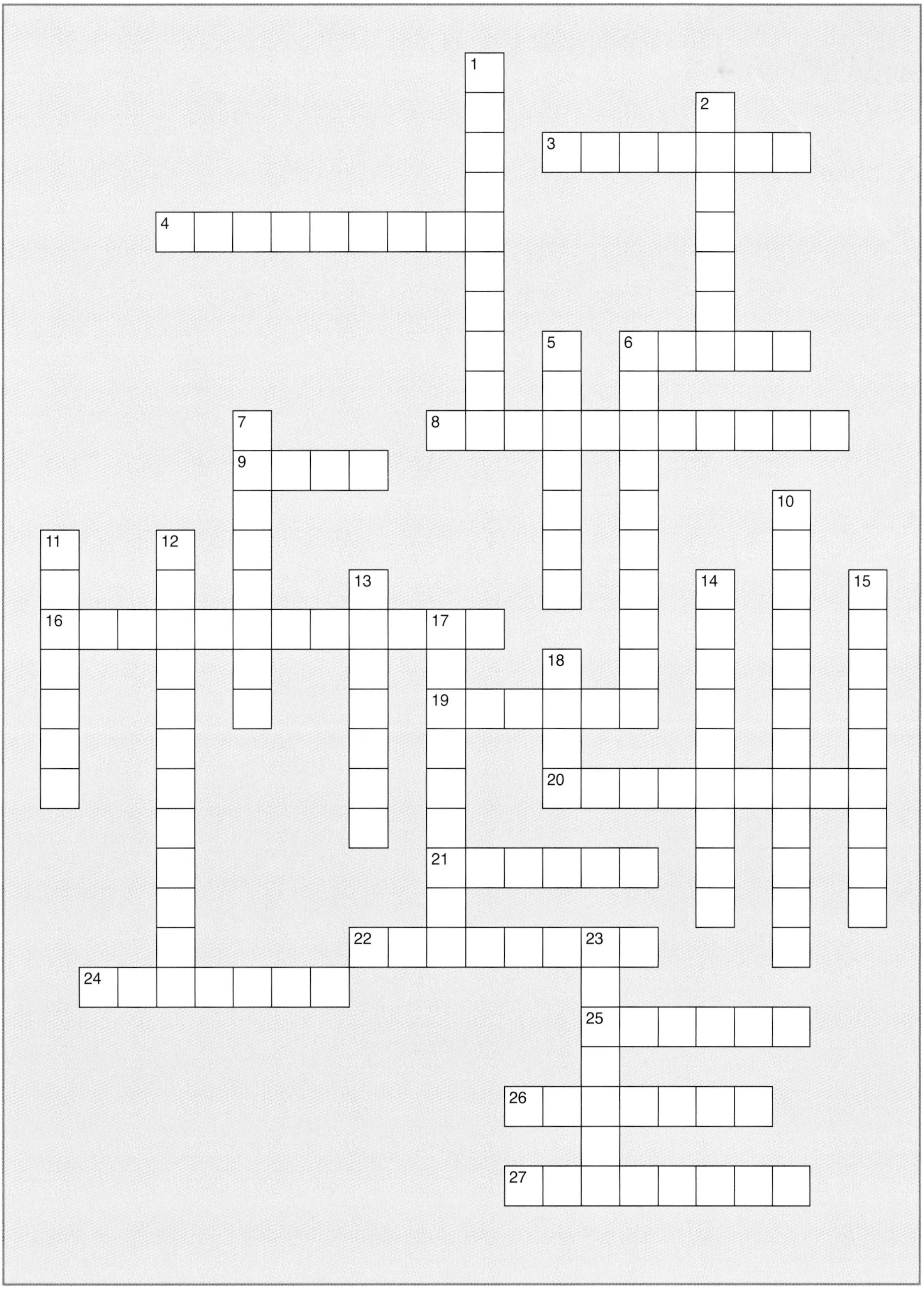
1
2
3
4
5
6
7
8
9
10
11
12
13
14
15
16
17
18
19
20
21
22
23
24
25
26
27

Unit 2, Exercise 9 — File 1

You work in the sales department of NewTech IT. Someone in the marketing department of Shopping Unlimited Retailers UK has asked you to come to their offices and tell them about your new software for customer mailing lists. After greetings and small talk, ask questions to get to know the company. Then tell them about your new software: it's the best product on the market. You can offer a 25% discount on your latest system, but you need to discuss bigger discounts with your boss first. (Only good customers get the bigger discount.)

Unit 2, Exercise 14 — File 2

You're the assistant marketing director for HealthyLife Assurance in the UK. You're working at the stand at a trade fair when you see a potential customer. Introduce yourself and offer assistance. Unfortunately you don't have any more brochures (today is the last day of the fair) but you can send some when you are back in the office. Take the customer's contact details and ask about the best way to get in touch (by email? a visit?).

HealthyLife Assurance

D.T. Kennison
Assistant Marketing Director

7 Garrison Road
Manchester M15 4BX
UK
++ 44 161 8720767
DTKennison@healthylife.com
www.healthylife.co.uk

Unit 3, Exercise 12 — File 3

Phone call 1

Today is Friday, 2 May. You are in London until Wednesday next week and would like to visit Gillian Browne in her office there. (You met at a recent trade fair and she is interested in your products.) If she's not there when you call, ask to speak to someone else that can help.

MAY

5 Monday	*9.00 M. Brooks* *11.30 Tramten* *15.15 Meet JT on Bond St*
6 Tuesday	*9.30 JT*
7 Wednesday	*13.00 meet T&R for lunch* *Meeting 14.30 (Sara 16.00?)* *20.30 BA456 Heathrow*
8 Thursday	*11.30 Mr Fisher*
9 Friday	

Phone call 2

You are the manager of the Italian ski resort Sci per Tutti. You wrote an email to ProfiSport yesterday asking for information about their latest ski equipment (catalogue and price list), and now somebody from the company is calling you to arrange a meeting. You are very busy next week but will be at the resort every day except Tuesday afternoon and Friday morning. (You might also have a lunch appointment on Thursday but are not 100% sure.)

Unit 4, Exercise 12 — File 4

Situation 1

You work in the call centre at Worldview Holidays PLC. You receive a call from a customer who would like information on package holidays to Japan. Ask him/her for information about dates, how many people will be travelling, and the customer's price range. Offer to send the customer your catalogue by email or post. Be sure to confirm the customer's contact details.

Situation 2

You work at a department store and you deal with customer information. You need information from your customer files in order to write a report. You can open the files, but unfortunately the text is scrambled and you can't read the information. You need to adjust the text setting, but you don't know how. Call your IT support agent to help you solve this problem.

> Call IT dept!
> Can enter password and open customer files but can't read the text – scrambled!
> Tried 'new start' twice but still same problem.
> How do I adjust the text setting?

Unit 5, Exercise 11	File 5

Write an email.

At a recent trade fair you met a new customer who is interested in information about your latest laptop. He/She gave you his/her business card and you promised to send the new brochure straight away. (You also saw him/her later at one of the trade fair cafés and had a quick lunch together.) Write your follow-up email (remember to attach the information he/she asked for) and give it to Partner B.

R Hoskins

TGT Holdings PLC

42 Syme Street
London WC1F 4RZ
RHoskins@tgt.com
www.tgt.com

Respond to an email.

Your name is F Ramos and you are the customer service manager at Siniad Ltd. You are arranging a seminar for 25 of your call centre agents and have called a hotel near your offices to find out about the menu and prices for a buffet lunch and coffee breaks. You now receive an email from the hotel (Partner B). Write an email back thanking Partner B for the information. You will try to make a decision by next week.

Unit 6, Exercise 10	File 6

Situation 1 (phone call)

You are calling RFH Catering Supplies to complain about a problem with your order. You've been charged double for the shipping fee on the last order of beer glasses and some of the glasses were also damaged during shipment. You have got a big party to service tomorrow, so you want RFH Catering to send the glasses straight away (it's urgent!) and to correct the invoice.

Invoice			
Contents	Cat no.	Unit Price	Total
100 beer glasses	VG3982	.62	62.00
100 wine glasses	WG7632	.75	75.00
100 wine glasses	WG6723	.81	81.00
200 small plates	RS6781	.55	110.00
		Subtotal	328.00
		Shipping	44.00
		Total	372.00

27 damaged
35 damaged
should be € 22

Situation 2 (face to face)

You are a guest at the Hotel Majestic and go to the hotel office to speak to the manager. You want to complain that your room is too noisy. The people in the next room have loud parties every night and you have not been able to sleep very well, so you are tired for your business meetings. Also, the hotel bed is very uncomfortable which makes it even more difficult to get some rest. Tell the manager to take action or you will move to another hotel.

Partner Files

Unit 2, Exercise 9 — File 1

You work in the marketing department at Shopping Unlimited Retailers UK and have asked someone from the sales department of NewTech IT to visit your company and tell you about their new software package for customer mailing lists. First greet the visitor and offer hospitality. Introduce him or her to any colleagues at the meeting and make small talk for 2 or 3 minutes before talking business. Be prepared to answer questions about your company. You are very interested in the software but you expect a 40% discount. You have another meeting to go to, but you want him or her to contact you tomorrow with an offer.

Unit 2, Exercise 14 — File 2

You are the personnel manager of Sunshine Juices, a company based in Florida. You are at a trade fair to find out about employee benefits, and especially life assurance programmes, for your staff in the UK branch of your company. You are not ready to buy anything yet. You just want information (perhaps some brochures?) to take back to your office. (Unfortunately you only have one business card with you – it's the last day of the fair – and you don't want to give it away.)

Sunshine Juices

S Ranger
Personnel Manager

2420 North Drive Av.
Orlando, Florida, FL 26214
Tel 77334709
Fax 77334719
s.ranger@sunshine.com

Unit 3, Exercise 12 — File 3

Phone call 1
Today is Friday 2 May. Your colleague – Gillian Browne – is not in the office today. But she has given you her diary and asked you to make appointments for her.

Week of 5 May

Monday	*4 p.m. dept meeting*
Tuesday	*8 a.m. breakfast meeting (until 10?)* *Meet Zak at 5 p.m.*
Wednesday	*John & Paulo – 10.30 (+ lunch?) p.m.* *Work on presentation (no calls)*
Thursday	*Annual meeting, Stockholm* *flight 8.30 a.m.*
Friday	*return flight 5.15 p.m.*

Phone call 2
You are a sales rep for ProfiSport, a company which sells sports equipment. The manager of the Italian ski resort Sci per Tutti emailed you yesterday and asked for a price list and catalogue for your latest ski equipment. Call her or him to say that you will send the information straight away. You will also be in the area at the end of next week and could visit on Thursday, if that's convenient. Perhaps you could take him/her out for lunch.

Unit 4, Exercise 12 — File 4

Situation 1
Your name is P Richardson and you are a regular customer with Worldview Holidays PLC. You phone their call centre to get information on package holidays to Japan. You'd like to go in September for 10 days with two friends and you don't want to pay more than ca €2,500 per person. You need the information quickly, so confirm your email address with the call centre agent.

Situation 2

You are an IT support agent for a call centre. You get a call from someone at a department store who is having trouble reading the customer information files. Ask him/her to explain how and when the problem happens. Then use the troubleshooting checklist to tell the person what to do. Make sure the customer follows and understands the steps. If the customer still can't read the files, offer to send a service technician at a convenient time.

Troubleshooting checklist

Problem:	*can't read files/scrambled text*
Action steps:	*click on 'format', then on 'text read'*
	click on 'text align' and press 'enter'
	it should be possible to read text now
Problem:	*has forgotten password*
Action steps:	

Unit 5, Exercise 11   File 5

Write an email.

You work at the Palace Hotel and one of your responsibilities is to arrange conferences and company events. You spoke to a new customer on the phone yesterday and want to write an email now to confirm what you agreed. He/She is planning a seminar at their offices (which are near your hotel) and wants to arrange a buffet lunch and two coffee breaks for 25 call centre agents. You told the customer that you will email him/her a menu and other information, including a price list. Write the email and give it to Partner A.

F. Ramos (f.ramos@siniadcorp.com)

Customer service manager, Siniad Ltd

Seminar for call centre agents – 25 people

lunch & 2 coffee breaks,
    21 September 1 p.m.

email menu and price list (pdf files)

Respond to an email.

Your name is R Hoskins and you work at a company called TGT Holdings PLC in London. You were at a trade fair recently and asked different people to send you information about their products. You have just received an email from one of the people you met there (Partner A). Write a response.

Unit 6, Exercise 10   File 6

Situation 1 (phone call)

You are the order agent for RFH Catering Supplies and a customer calls you to complain. Ask for details to solve the problem. Tell the customer that you will correct the invoice and then send him/her the new glasses by 5 p.m. today. Offer the customer a discount on the next order of glasses.

Invoice

Contents	Cat no.	Unit Price	Total
100 beer glasses	VG3982	.62	62.00
100 wine glasses	WG7632	.75	75.00
100 wine glasses	WG6732	.81	81.00
200 small plates	RS6781	.55	110.00
		Subtotal	328.00
		Shipping	44.00
		Total	372.00

Situation 2 (face to face)

You are the manager of Hotel Majestic and a guest comes to your office to complain. Note that your hotel is usually very quiet and suitable for business people, but this week there is a tennis tournament going on in your town and the hotel is full of younger people, who are unfortunately quite noisy. Give the guest something extra for his/her trouble such as free drinks, dinner or a voucher for a free room for his/her next stay.

Answer key

UNIT 1

page 5

1 customer satisfaction
customer convenience
customer-friendly
customer relations

page 6

(suggested answer)
1 *customer convenience*
2 saving customer profile
3 tracking site visits
4 easy navigation
5 efficient payment systems
5 good customer relations

2
1	successful	a	priority
2	priority	b	help/assistance
3	convenient	c	essential
4	efficient	d	convenient
5	essential	e	efficient
6	assistance	f	recommend
7	loyal		
8	recommend		

3 (suggested answers)
1 top quality products/goods and service
2 our good/competitive prices
3 free delivery and set-up/assembly/our online service/24-hour service
4 taking care of any customer problem within 48 hours
5 keep our customers coming back

page 7

4
1 receptionist
2 sales
3 representative
4 order entry clerk
5 shop assistant
6 cashier
7 teller
8 hotel
9 concierge
10 restaurant

5 (suggested answers)
1 A receptionist/A cashier/A shop assistant/A teller
2 A sales representative/A waiter/A shop assistant
3 An agent/A concierge/A bank officer/A teller
4 A sales manager/An agent
5 An order entry clerk/An agent/A sales representative
6 An agent/A manager/An officer

page 8

6 (suggested answers)
good telephone manner
good communication skills

ability to work well with customers/good customer service skills
ability to deal with complaints and problems
team work/ability to work in a team
being polite and diplomatic

7
1	N	5	N
2	P	6	N
3	N	7	P
4	P	8	P

page 9

8
1	*to be attentive*	5	prompt
2	to be in a hurry	6	impatient
3	rude	7	helpful
4	well informed	8	special

a attentive/patient/helpful/well informed/prompt
b rude
c uninformed/rude/impatient/unhelpful
d well informed
e rude/unhelpful/uninformed; well informed/polite/helpful

page 10

OUPTUT
1 D   2 D   3 A   4 D

UNIT 2

page 11

1 (suggested answers)
1	N	5	P
2	P	6	P
3	N	7	N
4	N		

page 12

2
1 a bank
2 a shop
3 a hotel
4 a company
5 a trade fair

1 How are you today?
2 let me know
3 Could you
4 May
5 meet you

1 b   2 c   3 d   4 c   5 a

3
1 must be
2 introduce
3 Nice
4 How was
5 May I take
6 you'd like
7 Would you

8 thanks so much
9 coming
10 trip

page 13

Greetings and introductions
Good morning. You must be … I'm …
Welcome to IGS.
It's nice to finally meet you face to face.
I'd like to introduce you to Annie Thomas.
Annie, this is Peter Masters …
Nice to meet you(, too).

Small talk questions
How was your flight?
And is this your first time in Brussels?

Offering hospitality
May I take your coat?
If you'd like to take a seat …
Would you care for coffee or tea?

Saying goodbye
Thanks so much for a good meeting.
Thanks for coming.
We'll be in contact by email …
Bye.
Have a nice trip!
So long for now.

4 1 introduce
2 finally
3 May
4 kind
5 like
6 care
7 get
8 contact
9 pleasure; journey
10 long

page 14

5 1 – c – E
2 – e – A
3 – a – F
4 – f – B
5 – b – D
6 – d – C

page 15

7 1 *Do*
2 *Do*
3 *Don't*; Do
4 Do; Don't
5 Don't
6 Don't; Do; don't
7 Do
8 Do

8 1 b
2 a
3 a
4 b
5 a
6 b

page 16

10 1 ☒
2 ☐?
3 ☒
4 ☒
5 ☑
6 ☒

(suggested answer)
Notes
interested customer
write him an email next week to thank him for
  stopping by the stand
follow-up to offer help again and to send out a new
  catalogue

11 1 introduce; ask
2 enjoying
3 anything
4 free; glad
5 brochure
6 put
7 mind; email

page 17

12 1 May/Could I ask/have your name?
2 Are you looking for anything special/in particular?
3 Please feel free to ask me any questions.
4 Can I interest you in a brochure?/Would you
  like/care for a brochure?
5 Would you like to put your name on the mailing
  list?/Would you like to be on our mailing list?
6 Do you mind if I take/Would you mind if I took
  your business card?
7 I'll email/phone you next week to see if I can
  help you with any of our products.

13 1 b
2 f
3 g
4 d
5 a
6 c
7 e

page 18

15 1 d
2 b
3 a
4 e
5 c

page 19

16 a *2*
b 9
c 4
d 1
e 6
f 7
g 3
h 5
i 8

UNIT 3

page 21

1 (suggested answers)

What went wrong
too much noise
poor listening
unhelpful
didn't connect the customer
shouting so that the customer can hear it

What went right
polite and friendly
helpful
patient
good listening
asked to repeat information
connected the customer to the right extension

1 May I help you?
2 you repeat that, please?
3 I'm afraid
4 Would you like me
5 Thanks for your call.

page 22

2
1 May I help you?
2 just a moment
3 would you like
4 Thanks for holding.
5 catch
6 I'm afraid
7 terribly sorry
8 Yes, certainly
9 I'll make sure
10 no problem

Message
Message for: Eva Lang
Caller: John Richards
Company: Customer Zone Software
Message: Call him as soon as possible today on 0044 7721 332558.

page 23

3
1 c
2 e
3 d
4 a
5 g
6 b
7 h
8 f

page 24

4
1 put; through
2 look up
3 speak up
4 cut off
5 got through to
6 get back to

5
1 hold
2 put
3 speak
4 May
5 leave
6 back to
7 afraid
8 repeat
9 I'll make sure
10 anything

page 25

7
1 Thomas
2 software
3 1
4 53
5 549822
6 price list

page 26

1 a
2 b
3 b
4 a
5 a

8 Yes, Peter Brenner followed all the steps.

a 2
b 6
c 9
d 8
e 4
f 1
g 7
h 5
i 1
j 7
k 10
l 3
m 4

page 27

9
1 g
2 f
3 b
4 d
5 e
6 c
7 a
8 h

10
1 h
2 d
3 k
4 a
5 l
6 f
7 i
8 b
9 j
10 e
11 g
12 c

page 28

11
1 c
2 d
3 e
4 a
5 b

13
1 confirm
2 holding
3 set up
4 appreciate
5 catch
6 convenient
7 once
8 would you
9 extension

The hidden word is: *courteous*

UNIT 4

page 30

Starter
1 24%
2 11%
3 16%
4 7%
5 62%

1 Caller 1 has called for help and caller 2 is placing an order.

Call 1
Customer: Mr Anderson
Customer interested in: help with bank's IT system
Follow-up: will call back in half an hour and maybe send out a technician

Call 2
Customer: Joe Walker, a regular customer
Customer interested in: placing an order
Follow-up: will send out order straight away

page 31

2 Call 1
1 It seems
2 Let me just
3 I understand; Is that right?
4 'll check; 'll call you
5 all right
6 Could I assist

Call 2
7 let me just pull up
8 do for
9 'll flag; straight away
10 Thank you

3
1 c
2 f
3 d
4 h
5 a
6 g
7 b
8 e

page 32

4
1 May I help you?
2 Could you give me your customer number, please?

3 I'd just like to confirm your contact details.
4 OK, let me just repeat that.
5 Is that right?
6 could I go over your order again?
7 Can I help you with anything else?

page 33

5 1 place
2 payment
3 dispatched
4 rush
5 give; catalogue
6 quote
7 invoice
8 overnight

6 (suggested answers)

1 I'm afraid I didn't quite catch that. Could you speak up a bit, please?
2 How can/may I help you today?/ assist you today?
3 I'm sorry I didn't quite understand/catch that.
4 How many packages would you like/are you interested in?
5 Would you mind giving me your address?/Could I/May I have your address?
6 Let me just read that back to you/repeat that. ... Can I help/assist you with anything else?
7 You should receive/get it by Tuesday *(be specific!)*. If you haven't got it by then, please give me a call. Thanks for your business. Bye for now.

page 34

7 1 b
2 a
3 b
4 b
5 a

The following sentences are in the conversation:
1 − 3 − 4 − 7 − 9 − 10 − 12

8 1 We just need to clarify a few things.
2 Is everything clear so far?
3 Could you explain what you've done so far?
4 That means you need to install some software.
5 What does OS stand for?
6 This is what I'm going to do.
7 Let me just talk you through the steps.

page 35

9 (Phrases in brackets also possible.)
1 Really? (Is that so?)
2 You don't say! (Really?/Oh, dear.)
3 Right. (I see.)
4 Of course. (Uh uh)

page 36

10 1 b
2 b
3 a
4 b
5 c
6 a

11 Across
1 clarification
5 satisfaction
6 explanation
8 delivery

a assistance
b explanation
c offer; payment

Down
2 assistance
3 payment
4 offer
7 order

UNIT 5

page 38

Starter
(suggested answers)

1 F
2 F
3 T
4 F
5 F
6 T
7 T
8 F
9 F

1 1 b
2 d
3 a
4 e
5 c

email: a, b, c, e
letter: d
You can tell because of the salutations and closes.

page 40

2 (suggested answers)

1 *Hi Hugo ... All the best*
2 Dear Walter ... Best wishes
3 Dear Janet and Mario ... Best wishes/Kind regards
4 Dear Ms Elan ... Yours sincerely or AmE: Sincerely (yours)
5 Dear Mr and Mrs Duchard... (Kind) regards/Best wishes
6 Dear Sir or Madam ... Yours faithfully or AmE: Sincerely (yours)

3 1 He probably doesn't know him very well.
2 At the Business Executive Conference.
3 A catalogue including prices.
4 Mr Bird will phone Mr Davis on Thursday to arrange a meeting.

page 41

4 1 b
2 f
3 d
4 a
5 e
6 g
7 c

1 It was a pleasure to speak to you (5e)
2 We are delighted to have you as a new customer (2f)
3 If you are satisfied with the results (6g)
4 I will pay you a visit personally (7c)
5 If you have any further questions (3d)
6 I look forward to seeing you next week (1b)
7 Thank you for choosing our company (4a)

page 42

5 Dear Mr Varley
b – f – a – d

Dear Mike
e – c – h – g

page 43

6 1 In regard to your phone call …
2 Thanks for your phone call this morning.
3 I am writing to let you know …
4 Just a quick email to let you know …
5 I am delighted to inform you …
6 I'm glad to tell you …
7 I would appreciate it if we could …
8 It'd be great if we could …
9 If you have any other questions, please don't hesitate to contact me.
10 I look forward to seeing you next week.
11 Let me know if you need any other help.
12 Looking forward to seeing you next week.

7 1 regard   5 hearing
2 pleased   6 would; convenience
3 of   7 reply
4 back   8 just

page 44

8 This email goes against the five Cs. It is unclear, incomplete, has too much unnecessary information, the language is not courteous enough and there are a lot of mistakes (spelling, punctuation, paragraphs in wrong order, salutation).

(suggested answer)

Dear Ms Jones

It was a pleasure to meet you recently at the Global Concepts Trade Fair. I hope you enjoyed the fair as much as I did.

As you requested, I've attached our latest price list. I would also like to send you our latest catalogue. Could you please confirm your postal address?

I would welcome the chance to find out more about your customer needs. I would like to phone you at the end of the week to arrange a meeting. Would Friday at 14.00 be convenient for you?

Thank you for your interest in Select Systems. I look forward to speaking to you soon.

Yours sincerely

9 1 c
2 a
3 b

email: a, b, (documents are 'attached')
letter: c (magazine is 'enclosed')

UNIT 6

page 48

2 do: 1, 4, 7, 8
don't: 2, 3, 5, 6

3 1 b (bank)
2 a (airport)
3 c (department store)

	complaint	response
Dialogue 1	poor service at bank	apologizes for service and staff; invites customer into the office to talk without interruption
Dialogue 2	flight has been cancelled	empathizes, explains reason and offers help
Dialogue 3	customer has been over-charged	offers to refund money and then agrees to exchange jumper

page 49

4 1 sorry; hear
2 seems; problem
3 let me apologize
4 I'm afraid
5 I'm sure; sort something out
6 let's see what we can do
7 appears; mistake
8 refund
9 problem; be glad

5 (suggested answers)
1 *There seems to be a misunderstanding.*
2 I'm afraid there's a problem/mix-up with your order.
3 It appears that some of the parts weren't included in the shipment.
4 It seems that your email didn't get through.
5 I'm afraid there's been a delay with your order. Your order should arrive by (early next week).
6 It appears that a mistake has been made.

page 50

6 1 b   4 c
2 e   5 a
3 d

7 1 Excuse me
2 seems to be
3 I'd like to say
4 I can see how
5 understand
6 Would you mind
7 straight away
8 make sure
9 inconvenienced
10 I'd be glad

8

What the receptionist did:	What the receptionist said:
1 *listened*	–
2 apologized	First of all, I'd like to say how sorry I am.
3 repeated	So, if I understand you correctly, ...
4 asked for	Would you mind giving me more details ... ?
5 took	I'll speak to housekeeping straight away.
6 offered	Since you've been so inconvenienced by this incident, I'd be glad to offer you ...

9
1 d 6 f
2 a 7 e
3 g 8 c
4 i 9 b
5 h

11
1 We are very concerned to hear
2 We very much regret
3 We assure you that we are doing everything we can
4 The problem has now been resolved
5 Once again, we apologize

a We are very concerned to hear that your order from last month has not reached you.
b We very much regret ...; Once again, we apologize for the inconvenience.
c We very much regret the frustration this has caused you.
d The delay was due to ...
e ... your order has been sent to you by overnight post.

12
1 c 4 e
2 d 5 b
3 a

13 (suggested answer)
These problems would be best handled by a phone call (to schedule a meeting) and then a personal visit. The problem-solving steps should be followed in a face-to-face meeting. Email should be used to follow-up the action points of the meeting.

Test yourself!

Across
3 appears
4 attentive
6 catch
8 responsible
9 ring
16 anything else
19 assist
20 delighted
21 afraid
22 make sure
24 confirm
25 go over
26 forward
27 hesitate

Down
1 appreciate
2 rapport
5 empathy
6 convenient
7 browsing
10 straight away
11 clarify
12 satisfaction
13 welcome
14 apologize
15 introduce
17 small talk
18 mind
23 regards

Transcripts

UNIT 2, EXERCISE 2

1

A Good morning, Ms Richards. How are you today?
B Fine, thanks. Ah, is Mrs Swift free at the moment? I have a quick question about my account.
A Yes, she's at the desk over there. Just go on over …

2

A Hello. May I help you with something?
B No, thank you. I'm just looking.
A Well, if you need help, just let me know.

3

A Hello, My name is Jaime Rodriguez. I have a reservation.
B One moment, please. Let me check. Ah yes. Could you just fill in this form, please, Mr Rodriguez?

4

A Hello. May I help you?
B Yes, I have an appointment with Ms Jamieson. My name is John Roberts.
A Roberts? Ah, yes. Please take a seat over there, Mr Roberts. I'll tell her you're here.

5

A Hello. May I help you?
B Yes, I'm with IBT Corporation. My name is Roger Allen. I have a few questions about your products.
A Ah, it's good to meet you, Mr Allen. I'm Sarah Levinson. So, how can I help you?

UNIT 2, EXERCISE 3

Frank   Good morning, you must be Peter Masters. I'm Frank Wepler. Welcome to IGS.
Peter   Thank you. It's nice to finally meet you face to face.
Frank   Yes, we've talked so much on the phone, I feel I know you already. Peter, I'd like to introduce you to Annie Thomas, our customer services manager. Annie, this is Peter Masters from TopForm, in Bristol.
Peter   Nice to meet you, Ms Thomas.
Annie   Nice to meet you, too.
Frank   So, if you'd just come this way …
Annie   How was your flight from Bristol?
Peter   It was fine. It even arrived a bit early.
Annie   And is this your first time in Brussels?
Peter   No, it's my third. I've been here a couple times as a tourist. I really like the city.
Frank   So, here we are. May I take your coat?
Peter   Oh, that's very kind of you.
Frank   If you'd like to take a seat …
Peter   Thank you.
Frank   Would you care for coffee or tea?
Peter   Tea would be nice, with two sugars.

       * * *

Peter   So, here's my taxi. Well, thanks so much for a good meeting. It was great to meet both of you.
Frank   The same for us. Thanks for coming. It was a very productive meeting. So, we'll be in contact by email as usual.

Peter   Yes, of course. Bye.
Annie   Have a nice trip! Bye.
Frank   So long for now.

UNIT 2, EXERCISE 10

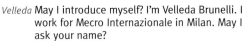

Velleda   May I introduce myself? I'm Velleda Brunelli. I work for Mecro Internazionale in Milan. May I ask your name?
Lewis   Lewis Gillan – I'm with Accutech UK. Nice to meet you.
Velleda   Pleased to meet you, too. So, Mr Gillan, how are you enjoying the trade fair?
Lewis   It's my first time here, actually. It's very interesting. Lots of good contacts. What about you?
Velleda   Oh, I'm enjoying it too. We're here every year and it's quite an important event for us. Well, then, are you looking for anything in particular?
Lewis   Right now I'm just browsing.
Velleda   OK, but please feel free to ask me any questions. I'd be glad to go over our products and try to find something suitable for your company.
Lewis   Thanks, that's very helpful. *(a few minutes later)* Well, thank you.
Velleda   Ah, can I interest you in a brochure? It has information about our company and our full range of products.
Lewis   Yes, thank you.
Velleda   Here you are. And we've got a new catalogue coming out next week. We're launching some exciting new products. Would you like to put your name on our mailing list?
Lewis   Yes, that would be good.
Velleda   Do you mind if I take your business card? I'll make sure you're on our list. And here's my card. I'll send you a quick email next week to see if I can help you with any of our products.
Lewis   That sounds fine. It was nice to meet you.
Velleda   The same here. Enjoy the rest of the fair.

UNIT 3, EXERCISE 1

Call 1

A Yeah?
B Hello. This is Marjorie Heighton. I'd like to confirm my appointment with Peter Gore.
A Um … sorry … what did you say?
B I'd like to confirm my appointment with Peter Gore, please.
A Well, this is the wrong number for that. Uh, wait. *(puts phone on hold)* Hello? Mrs … um … Hate …
B Heighton. Marjorie Heighton.
A Look, I'm not responsible for that. You'll have to call Peter's secretary.
B OK. Can you give me the phone number or connect me?
A Yeah, OK. Does anybody know Peter's extension?

Call 2

A Hello, Martha Greer speaking. May I help you?
B Hello. This is Donald Kraft. Could I speak to Anthony Smithson, please?

A Sorry, could you repeat that, please?

B Yes, this is Donald Kraft. I'd like to speak to Anthony Smithson.

A I'm afraid you've got the wrong extension, Mr Kraft. You need to speak to Mr Smithson's office. Would you like me to connect you?

B Yes, that would be great.

A OK, Mr Kraft. I'm putting you through now. Thanks for your call.

UNIT 3, EXERCISE 2

Call 1

12

Receptionist Good morning. Apex Industries. May I help you?

John Yes, this is John Richards from Customer Zone Software. I'd like to speak to Eva Lang, please. Could you put me through to her?

Receptionist Of course, just a moment, please. ... Oh, it seems that her line is engaged. Could you hold a moment? Or would you like to leave a message?

John I'd prefer to hold for just a minute or two. ...

Receptionist Mr Richards? Thanks for holding. I'm putting you through to Ms Lang's office now. If you get cut off for some reason, please get back to me.

John I'm sorry. Could you speak up a bit? I didn't quite catch that.

Receptionist Sure. I'm connecting you now to Ms Lang's office. If you don't get through, please ring again. We're having some problems with our phone system.

Call 2

13

Receptionist Good morning. Apex Industries.

John This is John Richards again. I'm afraid I got cut off when you tried to put me through.

Receptionist I'm terribly sorry about that.

John I really need to get through to Ms Lang this afternoon. Could I leave a message for her to ring me back as soon as possible?

Receptionist Yes, certainly, Mr Richards. Could I have your phone number, please?

John Yes, I'm calling from my mobile. It's 0044 7721 332558.

Receptionist Right. So, that's 0044 7721 332558. I'll make sure she calls you back today. Could I help you with anything else?

John Would it be possible to have her mobile number? Could you perhaps look it up for me?

Receptionist Yes, that's no problem. I've got it right here. It's 49 for Germany, then 156 8877944.

John Let me just repeat that. That's 49 156 8877944.

Receptionist That's right.

John OK thanks once again. Bye for now.

Receptionist You're welcome. Goodbye.

UNIT 3, EXERCISE 5

Maria Santos Group. How can I help?

14

Henry Hello. Could I have extension 226, please?

Maria I'm sorry, the line's engaged. Could you please hold? ... Sir, the line's free now. I'll put you through.

Henry Thanks.

Carlos Service department.

Henry I'd like to speak to Mr Martinez, please. Is he available at the moment?

Carlos May I ask who's calling?

Henry Henry Jones. I'm calling from GPT Ltd in London.

Carlos Just a moment please, Mr Jones. I'll see if he's available. ... Mr Jones? I'm afraid Señor Martinez is in a meeting. Would you like to leave a message?

Henry Yes, please ask him to get back to me as soon as possible. My number's 44 207 563361.

Carlos I'm afraid I didn't catch that. Could you repeat the number, please?

Henry Yes, it's 44 for the UK, then 207 563361.

Carlos OK, I'll make sure he gets the message. Is there anything else I can do for you?

Henry No, thanks.

Carlos Goodbye, then, Mr Jones. Thanks for calling.

Henry You're welcome. Goodbye.

UNIT 3, EXERCISE 7

Thomas Hello.

15

Brenner Hello, this is Peter Brenner from Infotech. Is that Mr Thomas?

Thomas Yes, it is.

Brenner Hello, Mr Thomas. I got your contact details from one of my colleagues. I'm calling to see if I could possibly interest you in our new line of customer tracking software.

Thomas Oh yes. What good timing. You know, we've been thinking about updating the way we keep customer information here and I've started making some enquiries about new software.

Brenner Really? I'm glad I've phoned you then. I'm in the area next week. Perhaps I could stop by your office and show you the latest software.

Thomas That sounds good. Could we set up a meeting on Wednesday, say, at one?

Brenner OK, that suits me fine. Let me just make sure I have the right address. That's 50 Azan Road, correct?

Thomas That's the main building. I'm actually across the street, at 53. Let me give you my mobile number, just in case. It's 07887 549822.

Brenner 887 ... I'm sorry, I didn't catch the last bit.

Thomas 549822.

Brenner 549822. OK, Mr Thomas, let me just confirm that. That's Wednesday at 1 p.m. and you're at 53 Azan Road. Mobile number 07887 549822.

Thomas That's right. In the meantime, could you give me an idea of a price range for the tracking software?

Brenner Sure. I'll email you a complete price list straight away and I'll also send you a PDF version of our brochure, if that's OK.

Thomas Yes, that would be very helpful. Thank you very much.

Brenner Is there anything else I can do for you before our meeting on Wednesday?

Thomas No, I think that's it.

Brenner OK. I look forward to seeing you on Wednesday, Mr Thomas.

Thomas Yes, see you then. Goodbye.

Brenner Goodbye.

UNIT 3, EXERCISE 10

16

Nathalie	Hello.
Susanne	Hello, may I speak to Nathalie Lawrence, please?
Nathalie	Speaking.
Susanne	Nathalie, this is Susanne Finster from Brand AG. We met at the trade fair last week.
Nathalie	Ah, yes. Right. How are you?
Susanne	Fine, thanks. Nathalie, I'm calling to see if we could set up a meeting. You wanted me to do a presentation on our services and I'll be in your area next week.
Nathalie	Next week? Let me just check my diary. What day exactly?
Susanne	Would Tuesday be convenient for you, at 9 a.m.?
Nathalie	Tuesday looks good, but I'm busy at nine. How about 11 o'clock instead?
Susanne	Sounds good. OK, Nathalie, that's Tuesday at 11 o'clock. I look forward to seeing you.
Nathalie	Same here. Thanks for calling. Bye.
Susanne	Bye.

UNIT 4, EXERCISE 1

Call 1
17

Customer	Hello.
Agent	Hello, is that Mr Anderson?
Customer	Yes, speaking.
Agent	This is Ashok Desai from NewTech Call Centre. I'm ringing because I got a message that you called our QuickHelp line. It seems that you need some assistance.
Customer	Oh, great. Yes, there's a bit of a problem with our IT system. When we try to view our customer records, the program crashes ...
Agent	Mr Anderson, let me just type this in ... one moment ... OK. Could you tell me when exactly it crashes?
Customer	Well, it's hard to tell what causes it. The normal screen comes up and asks you to type in the name first, then hit return, then type in the password. It seems OK at first, the new page comes up, then there's a funny clicking noise like the computer's trying to do something. This goes on quite a long time, then the screen just freezes.
Agent	OK, so, as I understand it, the problem begins with entering the password. Is that right?
Customer	Yes, that's right.
Agent	And how long have you had this problem?
Customer	Well, I've only tried it twice but then thought I'd better call you. So, when can you take care of this? Our work depends on the system being up and running all the time.
Agent	Yes, I can understand how important it is. I think we can send someone out to you this afternoon. I'll check the service technicians' schedule and I'll call you back in half an hour. Does that sound all right?
Customer	That sounds good.
Agent	Could I assist you with anything else today?
Customer	No, but thanks for asking. I'll be waiting for you to ring back.

Call 2
18

Agent	Good afternoon, Media Concepts. Gerry speaking. How can I help you?
Customer	Hello, I'd like to place an order, please. The name's Joe Walker. I'm already a regular customer.
Agent	Could I have your account number, please?
Customer	Mmm, yes, it's 55878.
Agent	55878 ... One moment, let me just pull up your customer file on my screen. Right. So, Mr Walker, what can I do for you?
Customer	I'd like to place an order for some spare parts and was wondering if it would be possible to receive them by Thursday? It's quite urgent.
Agent	Well, if the items are in stock, it should be no problem to send them out straight away. What exactly would you like to order? Could you give me the first order number, please?
Customer	OK, that's EJT53021. I'd like two of them. And the other order number is ... EJS36899. I need eight.
Agent	Was that EJS for Sam?
Customer	Right.
Agent	OK, let me repeat that. EJT for Thomas 53021, two items. And EJS for Sam 36899, eight items. Is that correct?
Customer	That's right. Are they in stock?
Agent	Yes, they are. I'll flag your order as urgent so that the items will be sent out straight away. You should receive the order in a couple of days, and definitely by Thursday.
Customer	Sounds good.
Agent	Can I help you with anything else today?
Customer	No, that's all for today, thank you.
Agent	OK, Mr Walker, thank you for your order. Goodbye.

UNIT 4, EXERCISE 7

20

Operative	Hello. Susanne speaking. How can I help you?
Customer	Hello. I hope I'm at the right place. I just got a new MP3 player – the i-go – and I can't seem to get it to work. I'm trying to install the software and it just won't work.
Operative	OK, first of all, is that the i-go mini or the i-go maxi?
Customer	The mini.
Operative	Right. So what exactly is the problem? Could you explain what you've done so far?
Customer	Well, I put in the CD to install the software and it seemed to work. *(Right.)* But now I can't open the window. *(OK.)* There's some message about something to do with the system and a number.
Operative	I see. It could be a systems requirement problem.
Customer	Sorry, what does that mean?
Operative	Well, the systems requirement for the i-go is OS 10 version 10.1.4. That means you need to have that version or a more recent one on your computer or you can't run the software for the i-go.
Customer	I see.
Operative	So, could you tell me which operating system you have on your computer?

Customer	No, sorry. I'm afraid I'm not very good with computers, as you can tell. I got this i-go for Christmas and I didn't think it would be so difficult to use.
Operative	Oh, don't worry. We just need to clarify a few things, then you'll have no trouble. OK, do you see the green box on the upper left-hand corner of your screen? *(Uh huh.)* When you click on it you'll see a menu. The first item on the menu says 'about your computer'. Are you following me all right?
Customer	Yes.
Operative	OK, click on that and you'll see what operating system you have. Are you having any trouble seeing that? The letters OS followed by some numbers?
Customer	Ah … yes, uhm … it's OS 10.1. Is that what you mean?
Operative	That's right and we've found your problem. You need to upgrade your system before you can install the software for your i-go.
Customer	And how do I do that?
Operative	Oh, that's very easy. Let me just talk you through the steps …

* * *

Operative	So, that will take a while to download, but once it does, you can just use it to upgrade your system free of charge. Then you'll have no trouble installing the i-go software.
Customer	Great. Thanks so much.
Operative	You're welcome. By the way, have you registered with us?
Customer	No, I don't think so. Could you tell me more about that?
Operative	Well, if you register with us, we can activate your guarantee and you'll have two years of free service …

UNIT 4, EXERCISE 9

🔘 21

C	I left a message for the call centre manager to call me back. That was three days ago and I've heard nothing from him.
A	Really? I'm so sorry. Let me see if I can help you …
C	I've emailed your helpline three times, but the emails have all been returned.
A	You don't say! I'm sorry about that. We must have had a problem with our server. It seems to be working all right now though. How I can help you?
C	I'm having trouble with my television. It turns on and I can see the picture, but I can't seem to get any sound.
A	Right. OK, I'm going to need to ask you some questions …
C	Your product is very good, but I'd like more information on an upgraded model.
A	Of course. I think I can suggest something for you …

UNIT 5, EXERCISE 9

🔘 **Message 1**
22 Hello, my name is Laura Gough, that's G–O–U–G–H. I'm going to be in Liverpool next week and I'd like to make a reservation for a single room with a bath for two nights, um that's Tuesday and Wednesday night, I think the dates are the 5th to the 7th of May. Could you just

confirm the reservation in writing? You have my contact details in your file. Oh, and could you also send me a list of events like concerts and plays for those evenings? Thanks.

🔘 **Message 2**
23 Hello, I'm calling about your catering service. We're having an office party in two weeks' time for about 50 people and I wanted to see some menus and get your price list. Could you send something asap? You can contact me at Hsu – that's H–S–U – @htk_systems.com. I'll repeat that. That's Hsu@htk_systems.com. Thanks.

🔘 **Message 3**
24 Hello, this is Mark Stephens calling again. I need the specifications for the 830T laser printer. Do you think you could email them to me this afternoon? Thanks and talk soon.

UNIT 6, EXERCISE 3

🔘 **Dialogue 1**
25

Customer	Excuse me. I'd like to make a complaint.
Bank manager	Oh, I'm sorry to hear that. What seems to be the problem?
Customer	Your bank service is just awful. I was here last week to take care of some banking transactions. The line was very long since there was only one teller. I asked a bank employee to bring in another teller, but he said they were too busy with more important work. So it took me over an hour to get my business done. I'm going to change to the Clyde Bank!
Bank manager	First of all, let me apologize for the poor service and unhelpful member of staff. It seems that you went through a terrible time getting your business done. Why don't you come into my office where we can talk without any interruptions … ?

🔘 **Dialogue 2**
26

Customer	Excuse me. I've just noticed the flight to Manchester's been cancelled. Is there anything you can do? I've got to be there by 10 tomorrow. It's really important. I use your airline all the time. Is there anything you can do? Go via London or something?
Airline agent	We've got a lot of people in the same position I'm afraid, but don't worry. I'm sure we'll sort something out. So, let's see what we can do.

🔘 **Dialogue 3**
27

Customer	Excuse me. I bought this jumper at your shop yesterday. When I got home, I looked at the receipt and saw that you had overcharged me ten euros.
Floor manager	Oh, I'm so sorry. It appears that our shop assistant made a mistake. I'll be happy to refund your money.
Customer	Actually, I've also decided that the jumper is not really the right colour, so I'd like to exchange them for something in red or yellow.
Floor manager	That's no problem. I'll be glad to help you.

A–Z word list

A

	Your language
abbreviation [ə,briːviˈeɪʃn]	
ability [əˈbɪləti]	
to accept [əkˈsept]	
acceptable [əkˈseptəbl]	
according to [əˈkɔːdɪŋ tə]	
accountancy [əˈkaʊntənsi]	
accurate [ˈækjərət]	
to acknowledge [əkˈnɒlɪdʒ]	
to activate [ˈæktɪveɪt]	
to adjust [əˈdʒʌst]	
advantage, to take ~ of [,teɪk ədˈvɑːntɪdʒ əv]	
advert(isement) [ˈædvɜːt, ədˈvɜːtɪsmənt]	
to affect [əˈfekt]	
after-sales service [ˈɑːftəseɪlz sɜːvɪs]	
agent [ˈeɪdʒənt]	
aggressive [əˈgresɪv]	
aim [eɪm]	
to align [əˈlaɪn]	
alternative [ɔːlˈtɜːnətɪv]	
anger [ˈæŋgə]	
to annoy [əˈnɔɪ]	
to apologize [əˈpɒlədʒaɪz]	
appointment [əˈpɔɪntmənt]	
to appreciate [əˈpriːʃieɪt]	
approach, first ~ [fɜːst əˈprəʊtʃ]	
appropriate [əˈprəʊpriət]	
approximately [əˈprɒksɪmətli]	
to arrange [əˈreɪndʒ]	
to assist [əˈsɪst]	
assistance [əˈsɪstəns]	
assurance, life ~ [ˈlaɪf əʃʊərəns]	
to assure [əˈʃʊə]	
to attach [əˈtætʃ]	
attempt [əˈtempt]	
to attend [əˈtend]	
attention [əˈtenʃn]	
attention, to pay ~ to [peɪ əˈtenʃn tə]	
attentive [əˈtentɪv]	
audience [ˈɔːdiəns]	
automated [ˈɔːtəmeɪtɪd]	
available [əˈveɪləbl]	
average [ˈævərɪdʒ]	
to avoid [əˈvɔɪd]	
awareness [əˈweənəs]	

B

	Your language
background [ˈbækgraʊnd]	
base, customer ~ [ˈkʌstəmə beɪs]	
bellhop [ˈbelhɒp]	
benefit [ˈbenɪfɪt]	
bind, to be in a ~ [bi ɪn ə ˈbaɪnd]	
to block [blɒk]	
body language [ˈbɒdi læŋgwɪdʒ]	
bond [bɒnd]	
to browse [braʊz]	
business area [,bɪznəs ˈeəriə]	

C

	Your language
call, to receive a ~ [rɪˈsiːv ə kɔːl]	
cancellation [,kænsəˈleɪʃn]	
to capture [ˈkæptʃə]	
to care for [ˈkeə fə]	
care, to take ~ of [teɪk ˈkeər əv]	
carry [,kæri]	
to carry out [,kæri ˈaʊt]	
case, just in ~ [dʒʌst ɪn ˈkeɪs]	
cashier [kæˈʃɪə]	
to catch [kætʃ]	
catering [ˈkeɪtərɪŋ]	
to chew [tʃuː]	
clarification [,klærɪfɪˈkeɪʃn]	
to clarify [ˈklærəfaɪ]	
clerk [klɑːk]	
clue [kluː]	
to combine [kəmˈbaɪn]	
communication skills [kə,mjuːnɪˈkeɪʃən skɪlz]	
to compare [kəmˈpeə]	
compensation [,kɒmpənˈseɪʃn]	
competition [,kɒmpəˈtɪʃn]	
competitor [kəmˈpetɪtə]	
complaint [kəmˈpleɪnt]	
compliment [ˈkɒmplɪmənt]	
concept [ˈkɒnsept]	
concerned, to be ~ [bi kənˈsɜːnd]	
concise [kənˈsaɪs]	
to confirm [kənˈfɜːm]	
to connect [kəˈnekt]	
consignment [kənˈsaɪnmənt]	
contract [ˈkɒntrækt]	
convenience [kənˈviːniəns]	
convenient [kənˈviːniənt]	
convention [kənˈvenʃn]	
correspondence [,kɒrɪˈspɒndəns]	
courteous [ˈkɜːtiəs]	
courtesy [ˈkɜːtəsi]	
to crash [kræʃ]	
to create [kriˈeɪt]	
to cross-sell [,krɒs ˈsel]	
crucial [ˈkruːʃl]	
current [ˈkʌrənt]	
customer-centred [ˈkʌstəmə sentəd]	
customer-friendly [ˈkʌstəmə frendli]	
cut off, to get ~ [get ,kʌt ˈɒf]	

D

	Your language
database [ˈdeɪtəbeɪs]	
to deal with sb/sth [ˈdiːl wɪð]	
decision [dɪˈsɪʒn]	
definitely [ˈdefɪnətli]	
to defuse [,diːˈfjuːz]	
to delay [dɪˈleɪ]	
delay [dɪˈleɪ]	
delighted [dɪˈlaɪtɪd]	
to deliver [dɪˈlɪvə]	
delivery [dɪˈlɪvəri]	
demand [dɪˈmɑːnd]	
demanding [dɪˈmɑːndɪŋ]	
to demonstrate [ˈdemənstreɪt]	

Your language

department [dɪ'pɑ:tmənt]

department store
[dɪ'pɑ:tmənt stɔ:]

dependable [dɪ'pendəbl]

desk [desk]

development [dɪ'veləpmənt]

diplomacy [dɪ'pləʊməsi]

directory [də'rektəri]

disconnected, to get ~
[get ˌdɪskə'nektɪd]

discount ['dɪskaʊnt]

dismay, to my ~ [tə maɪ dɪs'meɪ]

to dispatch [dɪ'spætʃ]

dissatisfied, to be ~
[bi dɪs'sætɪsfaɪd]

to distract [dɪ'strækt]

distraction [dɪ'strækʃn]

due [dju:]

duty ['dju:ti]

duty, to go beyond the call of ~
[gəʊ bɪˌjɒnd ðə kɔ:l əv 'dju:ti]

E

edge [edʒ]

effective [ɪ'fektɪv]

efficient [ɪ'fɪʃnt]

empathy ['empəθi]

to enclose [ɪn'kləʊz]

encounter [ɪn'kaʊntə]

engaged, the line is ~
[ðə laɪn ɪz ɪn'geɪdʒd]

engagement [ɪn'geɪdʒmənt]

enquiry [ɪn'kwaɪəri]

to ensure [ɪn'ʃʊə]

equipment [ɪ'kwɪpmənt]

equivalent [ɪ'kwɪvələnt]

especially [ɪ'speʃəli]

essential [ɪ'senʃl]

to establish [ɪ'stæblɪʃ]

estimate ['estɪmət]

event [ɪ'vent]

excerpt ['eksɜ:pt]

to exchange [ɪks'tʃeɪndʒ]

exchange [ɪks'tʃeɪndʒ]

to exhale [eks'heɪl]

exhibit area [ɪgˌzɪbɪt 'eəriə]

to expect [ɪk'spekt]

to experience [ɪk'spɪəriəns]

explanation [ˌeksplə'neɪʃn]

extension [ɪk'stenʃn]

extensive [ɪk'stensɪv]

F

face to face [ˌfeɪs tə 'feɪs]

faithful ['feɪθfl]

familiar, to sound ~
[saʊnd fə'mɪliə]

fault [fɔ:lt]

feature ['fi:tʃə]

fee [fi:]

feedback ['fi:dbæk]

feeling ['fi:lɪŋ]

file [faɪl]

to fill in [ˌfɪl 'ɪn]

to flag [flæg]

flow chart ['fləʊ tʃɑ:t]

fluent ['flu:ənt]

to focus on ['fəʊkəs ɒn]

to follow ['fɒləʊ]

follow-through [ˌfɒləʊ 'θru:]

Your language

follow-up ['fɒləʊ ʌp]

free of charge [fri: əv tʃɑ:dʒ]

to freeze [fri:z]

frequent ['fri:kwənt]

to frown [fraʊn]

frustration [frʌ'streɪʃn]

G

to generate ['dʒenəreɪt]

to get back to [ˌget 'bæk tə]

to get through [ˌget 'θru:]

to go over [ˌgəʊ 'əʊvə]

to go on over [ˌgəʊ 'ɒn əʊvə]

grateful ['greɪtfl]

grooming ['gru:mɪŋ]

guarantee [ˌgærən'ti:]

H

hand-held computer
[ˌhændheld kəm'pju:tə]

to handle ['hændl]

to hang up [ˌhæŋ 'ʌp]

helpline ['helplaɪn]

to hesitate ['hezɪteɪt]

highlight ['haɪlaɪt]

high-tech [ˌhaɪ 'tek]

to hold [həʊld]

hold, to put on ~ [pʊt ɒn 'həʊld]

hospitality [ˌhɒspɪ'tæləti]

house, open ~ [ˌəʊpən 'haʊs]

hurry, to be in a ~ [bi ɪn ə 'hʌri]

I

ice, to break the ~ [ˌbreɪk ði 'aɪs]

to ignore [ɪg'nɔ:]

immediately [ɪ'mi:diətli]

impact ['ɪmpækt]

impatient [ɪm'peɪʃnt]

impression [ɪm'preʃn]

impressive [ɪm'presɪv]

incentive [ɪn'sentɪv]

incident ['ɪnsɪdənt]

inconvenienced, to be ~ by
[bi ˌɪnkən'vi:niənst baɪ]

to inhale [ɪn'heɪl]

insecure [ˌɪnsɪ'kjʊə]

to install [ɪn'stɔ:l]

instant ['ɪnstənt]

instantly ['ɪnstəntli]

instead [ɪn'sted]

insulting [ɪn'sʌltɪŋ]

intention [ɪn'tenʃn]

to interrupt [ˌɪntə'rʌpt]

interruption [ˌɪntə'rʌpʃn]

introduce, to ~ oneself
[ˌɪntrə'dju:s wʌnself]

invisible [ɪn'vɪzəbl]

invitation [ˌɪnvɪ'teɪʃn]

invoice ['ɪnvɔɪs]

item ['aɪtəm]

J

jargon ['dʒɑ:gən]

jumper ['dʒʌmpə]

L

latest ['leɪtɪst]

latter ['lætə]

to launch [lɔ:ntʃ]

leaflet ['li:flət]

to lease [li:s]

least, the ~ [ðə 'li:st]

location [ləʊ'keɪʃn]

Your language

long, so ~ for now
[səʊ 'lɒŋ fə naʊ]
long-term [ˌlɒŋ 'tɜːm]
to look up [ˌlʊk 'ʌp]

M
mail, junk ~ ['dʒʌŋk meɪl]
mailing list ['meɪlɪŋ lɪst]
to make sure [ˌmeɪk 'ʃʊə]
manual ['mænjuəl]
manufacturing [ˌmænju'fæktʃərɪŋ]
to matter ['mætə]
meantime, in the ~
[ɪn ðə 'miːntaɪm]
to memorize ['meməraɪz]
to mention ['menʃn]
mind, to change my ~
[ˌtʃeɪndʒ maɪ 'maɪnd]
misleading [ˌmɪs'liːdɪŋ]
misunderstanding
[ˌmɪsʌndə'stændɪŋ]
mix-up ['mɪks ʌp]
moreover [mɔːr'əʊvə]
mouse, to be a ~ click away
[bi ə 'maʊs klɪk əweɪ]
to network ['netwɜːk]

N
news flash ['njuːz flæʃ]
nowadays ['naʊədeɪz]

O
to offer ['ɒfə]
once [wʌns]
operating system
['ɒpəreɪtɪŋ sɪstəm]
operator ['ɒpəreɪtə]
opinion [ə'pɪniən]
order entry clerk
[ˌɔːdər 'entri klɑːk]
order, to place an ~
[ˌpleɪs ən 'ɔːdə]
otherwise ['ʌðəwaɪz]
outcome ['aʊtkʌm]
outlook ['aʊtlʊk]
to overcharge [ˌəʊvə'tʃɑːdʒ]
overlooked, to get ~
[get ˌəʊvə'lʊkt]
oversight ['əʊvəsaɪt]
overview ['əʊvəvjuː]
to overwhelm [ˌəʊvə'welm]

P
package holiday
['pækɪdʒ hɒlədeɪ]
paragraph ['pærəɡrɑːf]
particular [pə'tɪkjələ]
partnership ['pɑːtnəʃɪp]
password ['pɑːswɜːd]
patient ['peɪʃnt]
people skills ['piːpl skɪlz]
perception [pə'sepʃn]
to perform [pə'fɔːm]
pleasant ['pleznt]
pleasure, my ~ [maɪ 'pleʒə]
point [pɔɪnt]
policy ['pɒləsi]
polite [pə'laɪt]
position [pə'zɪʃn]
possibility [ˌpɒsə'bɪləti]
postcode ['pəʊstkəʊd]

Your language

potential [pə'tenʃl]
prepared, to be ~ [bi prɪ'peəd]
pressure, under ~ [ˌʌndə 'preʃə]
to pretend [prɪ'tend]
preview ['priːvjuː]
priority [praɪ'ɒrəti]
to process ['prəʊses]
productive [prə'dʌktɪv]
profit ['prɒfɪt]
promise ['prɒmɪs]
promotional [prə'məʊʃənl]
prompt [prɒmpt]
prompt, to be ~ in [bi 'prɒmpt ɪn]
promptly ['prɒmptli]
proud, to be ~ of [bi 'praʊd əv]
to provide [prə'vaɪd]
to pull up [ˌpʊl 'ʌp]
punctuation [ˌpʌŋktʃu'eɪʃn]
to put through [ˌpʊt 'θruː]

Q
questionnaire [ˌkwestʃə'neə]
quote [kwəʊt]

R
range [reɪndʒ]
rapport [ræ'pɔː]
rate [reɪt]
to rate [reɪt]
to reach [riːtʃ]
to react [ri'ækt]
to realize ['rɪəlaɪz]
receipt [rɪ'siːt]
receiver [rɪ'siːvə]
to recommend [ˌrekə'mend]
to refer (to) [rɪ'fɜː tə]
reference ['refərəns]
refund ['riːfʌnd]
to refund [rɪ'fʌnd]
regard, in ~ to [ɪn rɪ'ɡɑːd tə]
regional ['riːdʒənl]
to register ['redʒɪstə]
register ['redʒɪstə]
to regret [rɪ'ɡret]
regular ['reɡjələ]
relocation [ˌriːləʊ'keɪʃn]
to renew [rɪ'njuː]
to replace [rɪ'pleɪs]
replacement [rɪ'pleɪsmənt]
report [rɪ'pɔːt]
request [rɪ'kwest]
required, to be ~ [bi rɪ'kwaɪəd]
to resolve [rɪ'zɒlv]
resort [rɪ'zɔːt]
responsible, to be ~ for
[rɪ'spɒnsəbl]
responsibility, to take ~
[teɪk rɪ,spɒnsə'bɪləti]
rest, to get ~ [get 'rest]
retail ['riːteɪl]
revenue ['revənjuː]
to review [rɪ'vjuː]
rude [ruːd]
to ruin ['ruːɪn]
runaround, to give sb the ~
[ɡɪv ðə 'rʌnəraʊnd]
to rush [rʌʃ]
rush order [rʌʃ 'ɔːdə]

Your language

Your language

S

salutation [ˌsælju'teɪʃn]
satisfaction [ˌsætɪs'fækʃn]
schedule ['ʃedjuːl]
scrambled ['skræmbld]
screen [skriːn]
script [skrɪpt]
security precaution
 [sɪ'kjʊərəti prɪˌkɔːʃn]
selection [sɪ'lekʃn]
service ['sɜːvɪs]
to service ['sɜːvɪs]
service, to give good/bad ~
 [gɪv ˌgʊd, ˌbæd 'sɜːvɪs]
service line ['sɜːvɪs laɪn]
to set up [ˌset 'ʌp]
setting, text ~ ['tekst setɪŋ]
sharply ['ʃɑːpli]
shipment ['ʃɪpmənt]
to sign up [ˌsaɪn 'ʌp]
signal, engaged ~
 [ɪnˌgeɪdʒd 'sɪgnəl]
to sip [sɪp]
to slam down [ˌslæm 'daʊn]
small talk ['smɔːl tɔːk]
to soften ['sɒfn]
solution [sə'luːʃn]
spare part [ˌspeə 'pɑːt]
to speak up [ˌspiːk 'ʌp]
specific [spə'sɪfɪk]
specification [ˌspesɪfɪ'keɪʃn]
speedy ['spiːdi]
spellchecker ['speltʃekə]
to stand for ['stænd fə]
standard ['stændəd]
startling ['stɑːtlɪŋ]
statement ['steɪtmənt]
stock, to be in ~ [bi ɪn 'stɒk]
to stop by [ˌstɒp 'baɪ]
straight away [streɪt ə'weɪ]
strong [strɒŋ]
subscriber [səb'skraɪbə]
success story [sək'ses ˌstɔːri]
successful [sək'sesfl]
to suggest [sə'dʒest]
suggestion [sə'dʒestʃən]
to suit [suːt]
suitable ['suːtəbl]
to sum up [ˌsʌm 'ʌp]
supervisor ['suːpəvaɪzə]
survey ['sɜːveɪ]
system requirement
 [sɪstəm rɪ'kwaɪəmənt]

T

tact [tækt]
to take the time [teɪk ðə 'taɪm]
team [tiːm]
technician [tek'nɪʃn]
telephone manner
 ['telɪfəʊn mænə]
teller ['telə]
tip [tɪp]
tool [tuːl]
totally ['təʊtəli]
touch, to get in ~ [get ɪn 'tʌtʃ]
tournament ['tʊənəmənt]
to track [træk]
trade fair ['treɪd feə]
transaction [træn'zækʃn]
transfer ['trænsfɜː]
to transfer [træns'fɜː]
trend [trend]
troubled, to look ~ [lʊk 'trʌbld]
troubleshooting ['trʌblʃuːtɪŋ]
turn-around time ['tɜːn əraʊnd ˌtaim]

U

unacceptable [ˌʌnək'septəbl]
uncomfortable [ʌn'kʌmftəbl]
unique selling point (USP)
 [juˌniːk 'selɪŋ pɔɪnt]
unsatisfactory [ˌʌnˌsætɪs'fæktəri]
up and running [ʌp ən 'rʌnɪŋ]
to update [ʌp'deɪt]
to upgrade [ʌp'greɪd]
urgent ['ɜːdʒənt]
used, to get ~ to [get 'juːstə]
useless ['juːsləs]

V

valued ['væljuːd]
view, point of ~ [ˌpɔɪnt əv 'vjuː]
voicemail ['vɔɪsmeɪl]
voucher ['vaʊtʃə]

W

to waste [weɪst]
well-known [ˌwel 'nəʊn]
wronged [rɒŋd]

Y

to yell at sb ['jel ət]

Useful phrases and vocabulary

Basic socializing

Greetings and introductions
Good morning. You must be …
It's nice to finally meet you face to face.
– It's good/nice to meet you, too.
I'd like you to meet …
Anke, this is …
I'd like to introduce you to …
May I introduce myself? I'm …
– Nice to meet you. I'm …

Small talk questions
How was your trip (AmE)/journey (BrE)/flight?
Did you find us OK?
Did you have any trouble finding us?
And is this your first time in Brussels?
So, have you ever been to Brussels before?
So, how's your hotel? Everything OK?
Great weather, isn't it?
How was the weather in London?
Oh, are you interested in tennis?

Offering hospitality
May I take your coat?
Let me help you with that.
– Oh, that's very kind of you.
So, if you would like to take a seat …
Please take a seat.
– Thank you.
Would you care for coffee or tea?
Would you like some coffee or tea?
– Yes, please. Tea would be nice.
Can I get you some mineral water?
– No, thank you.
Can I get you something else? Juice, perhaps?

Saying goodbye
Thanks for stopping by.
Thanks for a good meeting.
It was great to meet (both of) you.
Have a good trip (AmE)/journey (BrE).
So long for now.
Goodbye./Bye.

General conversation

Asking for clarification
I'm sorry, but I didn't (quite) catch that/understand
  you exactly.
Could we go over that once more?
Could you repeat that, please?
Could you speak a bit slower/more slowly, please?

Making suggestions
Why don't you/we … ?
Don't/Wouldn't you agree that … ?
Isn't it a better idea to … ?
It makes a good/bad impression if you …

Responding to suggestions
That's right. / I agree.
I see your point.
I disagree because …
I don't agree. I would …

Customer meetings
Thanks for coming today.
As I understand it, you'd like to discuss …
I've done some research into your company. It
  seems you … . Is that right?
So, that was my suggestion. Is that suitable for you?
  I'd like to get your feedback.
Let's go over the action points once more. I want to
  be sure we agree.
I'll see what we can do.

Trade fairs

Starting a conversation
Excuse me, may I help you?
– No, thanks. I'm just looking/browsing.
How can I help you?
May I introduce myself? I'm …
– Nice/Pleased to meet you. I'm …
Could I ask your name?
– My name's …
How are you enjoying the fair?
– It's very interesting. It's a good chance to network.

Talking business

Are you looking for anything special/in particular?
– I'm looking for/interested in …
Could I offer you/interest you in … ?
– Yes, I'd like to have your latest brochure/
   catalogue/price list.
Please feel free to ask me any questions.
Would you mind if I … phoned/emailed/contacted
   you?
May I give you my card?
– Of course. And here's mine. I look forward to
   hearing from you …

Ending the conversation

It was so nice to meet you.
I hope you enjoy the fair.
– Thanks, it was a pleasure. I appreciate your help.

Presentations

Welcoming/Introducing

I'd like to welcome you to …
Thank you for coming today.
My name's …
I work for … and I'm in charge of/responsible for …

Introducing the subject

I'd like to give you a short preview of my
   presentation …
We'd like to introduce/show you/help you get to
   know our latest …

Describing products and services

Our product/service range includes …
The special highlights are …

Explaining the unique selling points (USPs)

We stand out from our competitors because …
Our USPs are …

Giving promotional information

Please feel free to pick up/take a brochure/leaflet/
   free sample.
We've got our promotional information and samples
   available here.

Offering incentives to try a product

I'd like to offer a special introductory price.
We can offer you a discount if you order today.

Offering follow-up

I'll be glad/pleased to send you … by next Monday.
I'll be in contact/touch with you in two weeks.
I/We look forward to doing business with you.

Inviting/appreciating new customers

We'd be pleased/glad to have you as a new
   customer.
We'd welcome the chance to do business with your
   company.

Summarizing

I'd just like to sum up the main points of today's
   presentation.
Thank you for your kind attention.

Telephoning

Identifying yourself (person called)

Good morning. Apex industries.
Hello, Martha Greer speaking. How can/may I help
   you?

Identifying yourself (caller)

Hello, my name is … . I'm with GPT Ltd in London.
This is Joan Everts from Everts, Samuels, and Barker.
Hello, I'd like to introduce myself.
I'm calling to …

Getting through

I'd like to speak to John, please.
Could you put me through to John, please?
– Of course, one moment please.
– Thanks for holding/waiting. I'm putting you
   through to John's office now.

Messages

Would you like to leave a message?
– That's OK. I'll call back later.
   Could I leave her a message to ring me back as
   soon as possible?
– I'll make sure she gets your message straight
   away.
   I'll make sure he calls you back today.

Showing attention

I'll just write that down.
Let me just make a note of that.
I've got your customer file right in front of me.
I'm checking your file as we speak.

Confirming information

Can I just go over/confirm the details again?
Let's go over it again to be sure of the details.

Explaining action

I'll be glad to send this out to you today.
You should receive it by …

Showing follow-up

I'll check on that information with my colleague and
  call you back in two hours.
I'll make sure that he/she calls you back today.

Finishing the call

Could I help/assist you with anything else today?
Can I take care of anything else for you?
Is there anything else I can help you with today?
I appreciate you taking the time to talk to me.
Many thanks for calling us.

Making arrangements

Asking for an appointment

Could we schedule an appointment?
Are you available/free on Monday?
Does next Thursday suit you?
How about 2 p.m. on Tuesday?

Agreeing on a time

Just let me check my diary/planner.
Yes, Tuesday is fine with me.
Sounds good. Tuesday at 2 p.m. then.

Suggesting a new time

I'm sorry, but I've got another engagement.
How about Tuesday morning instead?
Actually, Thursday morning would work out/be
  better for me.

Confirming

OK, we'll see each other next Thursday at 11.00 at
  your office.
Could you confirm the details in an email?
Here is my mobile number in case you need to
  reach me.
I look forward to seeing you (then).

Call centre phone calls

Offering assistance

How can I help you today?
What can I do for you?

Understanding customers

I see. So, as I understand it, … . Is that correct?
Let me just repeat that.

Confirming details

Could I just have your name and address, please?
I'd just like to confirm your contact details.
Could I go over your order again?

Making promises and keeping them

Your order will go out overnight today.
I'll call you back in half an hour.
I will personally make sure …

Agreeing on action

Does that sound all right?
Do you have any other questions?
I hope this is to your satisfaction.

Following up and following through

I'll ring you when the technician has finished the
  repair work to make sure everything is all right.

Troubleshooting

So, what exactly is the problem?
Could you explain the problem in more detail?
Could you explain what you've done so far?
Let me just talk you through the steps.
Do you follow that so far?
Do you have any questions so far?
Can you see that all right?
Is everything clear up to now?
– What exactly does OS stand for?
– What do you mean exactly?
– Sorry, what does that mean?
That means you need to have …
In other words, you need to have …
This is what I'm going to do: …

Problems and complaints

Apologizing

First of all, I'm so/terribly sorry about that.
I apologize for …
Let me apologize …

Clarifying the information

Could you tell me exactly what happened?
Could you explain a bit more …?
Do you mind if I just go over that again …?

Listening carefully
I'll just make a few notes as you speak.
I'm just taking this down.

Showing empathy
I understand./I see what you mean.
I would feel the same way.
I can understand the reason for your complaint.
What a difficult situation this puts you in.

Taking responsibility
There seems to be a misunderstanding.
It appears that your order got overlooked.
I'm afraid there has been some sort of mix-up.
It looks like an oversight on our part.
It seems (that) the order was not handled promptly
   enough.
It appears (that) a mistake has been made.

Saying how and when the problem will be solved
I'll take care of this for you at once.
I'll get back to you straight away.
You'll receive (a refund/replacement) by tomorrow ...
I'm sure we can find a solution.
I'd be glad to offer you ... to make up for this
   inconvenience.
This should be resolved by the end of today.

Offering an alternative
If this solution does not meet your needs, then I
   can suggest ... as an alternative.
I'll look into other possibilities by ...

Summarizing the discussion
What we have decided is ...
Our action plan is ...
I'd like to go over this once more to make sure we
   agree.

Assuring the client of follow-up
I'll get back to you in/by ...
I'll follow up to make sure that ...

Ending with a friendly, helpful tone
I hope you are satisfied with the outcome.
Thank you for bringing this to our attention.
Is there anything else I can help you with today?
Don't hesitate to ring again if there are any more
   problems.

Dealing with complaints in writing (formal)
We very much regret ...
We are very concerned to hear that ...
We assure you that we are doing everything
   we can ...
The problem has now been resolved.
Once again, we apologize for the inconvenience.
We (do) value your business and hope to keep you
   as a long-term customer.

Letter and email writing (formal/less formal)

Connecting with the reader
In reference to your letter/email of ...
In/With regard to your phone call ...
Further to our recent meeting ...
Re your letter/email of ...
Thanks for your phone call this morning.
I hope everything is going well.

Reason for writing
We are writing to confirm ...
I am writing to let you know ...
I would like to inform you ...
I'm just writing to tell you ...
I'd like to let you know ...
Just a quick email to let you know ...

Enclosures
Please find enclosed the price list you requested.
In the enclosed information packet, you will find
   product descriptions, ...
As you will see from the enclosed brochure, ...

Attachments
I'm sending you the current price list as an
   attachment.
I've attached the specifications as a pdf document.
Please complete the attached form and return it to
   us.
Here is the file you asked for.

Giving good news
We are pleased to say ...
I am delighted to inform you ...
I'm happy to tell you ...
I'm glad to tell you ...

Requests

We would be grateful if we could ...
I would appreciate it if we could ...
It'd be great if we could ...
Could you ... ?

Taking action

I will phone you/contact you ...
We would be delighted/pleased to assist you.
I'll get in touch with you/get back to you ...
I'd be glad to help out.

Concluding

If you have any further questions, please do not hesitate to contact me.
If you have any other questions, please contact me.
We look forward to hearing from/meeting you soon.
I look forward to seeing you next week.
Let me know if you need anything else/any other help.
Look(ing) forward to your reply/to hearing from you.
Look(ing) forward to seeing you next week.

Useful Verbs (in context)

to apologize	We apologize for the mix-up with the invoice.
to appreciate	We appreciate you as a valuable customer.
to assist	How can I assist you with your order today?
to assure	I can assure you that you will receive a refund by Friday.
to be grateful	We would be grateful if you could contact us soon.
to be in charge of	Can you tell me who is in charge of this account?
to be responsible for	I am responsible for (taking) all of your orders.
to care for sth	Would you care for a drink?
to catch	I didn't catch that. Could you say it again?
to confirm	Let me just confirm your contact details.
to deal with	I'll connect you with somebody who deals with that.
to follow through	We follow through on every customer request.
to follow up	I am writing to follow up on our phone call yesterday.
to get back to sb	I'll make sure she gets back to you by Friday.
to get through to	I'm sorry you were unable to get through to the helpdesk.
to go over	I'll go over it again to make sure it's clear.
to hold	Could you hold or would you prefer to leave a message?
to inconvenience	We hope you have not been inconvenienced by the delay.
to inform	Please inform us as soon as you receive the package.
to look into sth	I'll look into your question and call you back in two hours.
to put sb through	One moment, please. I'll put you through to the manager.
to recommend	I'd like to recommend a solution for all your business needs.
to regret	I regret that this has caused you so many problems.
to resolve	We will do everything possible to resolve the misunderstanding.
to schedule	Could we schedule a time to meet next week?
to stand out	We stand out from our competitors with our superior service.
to take care of sth	We try to take care of all complaints within 24 hours.
to take sth down	One moment, I just need to take down your address.
to talk sb through sth	I'll talk you through the steps to solve the problem.